# THE URIAH SYNDROME

## THE MISUSE AND ABUSE OF AUTHORITY IN THE CHURCH

Robert Dixon

ISBN 978-1-64471-873-5 (Paperback)
ISBN 978-1-64471-874-2 (Digital)

Copyright © 2019 Robert Dixon
All rights reserved
First Edition

All rights reserved. No part of this publication may be reproduced, distributed, or transmitted in any form or by any means, including photocopying, recording, or other electronic or mechanical methods without the prior written permission of the publisher. For permission requests, solicit the publisher via the address below.

Covenant Books, Inc.
11661 Hwy 707
Murrells Inlet, SC 29576
www.covenantbooks.com

*Whenever Moses held up his hand, Israel prevailed, and whenever he lowered his hand, Amalek prevailed. But Moses' hands grew weary, so they took a stone and put it under him, and he sat on it, while Aaron and Hur held up his hands, one on one side, and the other on the other side. So his hands were steady until the going down of the sun.*
—Exodus 17:11–12

To the one who has held up my hands for over thirty years, whenever they grew weary and I could not— to my beautiful wife and faithful friend, Marsha.

# Acknowledgment

I would also like to acknowledge and thank my children, Joshua, Caleb, Kathryn, Kelsey, and Joanna, who have extended patience, love, forbearance, and much encouragement toward me as I spent countless hours preparing the material in this book. I am most grateful they have been able to prevail the storm of their own church experience while growing up and, to their credit and God's grace, remain steadfast in their love of Jesus, their faith in God, and their hope for His church. All of you have proven the Scripture true.

> Behold, children are a heritage from the LORD, the fruit of the womb a reward. Like arrows in the hand of a warrior are the children of one's youth. Blessed is the man who fills his quiver with them! (Psalm 127:3–5)

Additionally, my family and I are very aware that without the devoted intercession and practical love and kindness of my sister-in-law, Patti Brown, toward each one of us, we would all be worse for the wear. We are so very grateful and love you like family.

To my brothers in battle, Buddy and Steve, who consistently demonstrated integrity, tenacity, and fearlessness as we fought the "good fight" side by side—holding firm, never flinching, even in the face of intimidation and great loss. What courageous brothers in Christ you are!

Finally, I would like to acknowledge Brian Sterling, who excelled in his gift of editing and transformed a manuscript originally "written like you talk" into one more readable and accessible. Thank you for your dedication and perseverance to bring this project to completion.

*In keeping silent about evil, in burying it so deep within us that no sign of it appears on the surface, we are implanting it, and it will rise up a thousandfold in the future. When we neither punish nor reproach evildoers, we are not simply protecting their trivial old age, we are thereby ripping the foundations of justice from beneath new generations.*

—Alexander Solzhenitsyn,
The Gulag Archipelago

# Foreword

"We know that ministers are subject to the same frailties and imperfections with other men. We know too that a love of preeminence and of power is not only natural to them, in common with others; but that this principle, very early after the days of the Apostles, began to manifest itself as the reigning sin of ecclesiastics and produced first prelacy and afterward popery, which has so long and so ignobly enslaved the church of Christ. Does not this plainly show the folly and danger of yielding undefined power to pastors alone? Is it wise or safe to constitute one man a despot over a whole church? Is it proper to entrust to a single individual the weighty and complicated work of inspecting, trying, judging, admitting, condemning, excluding, and restoring without control? Ought the members of a church to consent that all their rights and privileges in reference to Christian communion should be subject to the will of a single man as his partiality, kindness, and favoritism on the one hand; or his caprice, prejudice, or passion, on the other, might dictate? Such a mode of conducting the government of the church to say nothing of its unscriptural character is in the highest degree, unreasonable, and dangerous. It can hardly fail to exert an influence of the most injurious character, both on the clergy and laity. It tends to nurture in the former, a spirit of selfishness, pride, and ambition; and instead of ministers of holiness, love, and mercy, to transform them into ecclesiastical tyrants. While its tendency, with regard to the latter, is gradually to beget in them a blind, implicit submission to clerical domination. The ecclesiastical encroachments and despotism of former times already alluded to read us a most instructive lesson on this subject. The fact is, committing the whole government of the Church to the hands of pastors alone, may be affirmed to carry in it some of the worst seeds of popery; which, though under the administration of good men, they may not at once lead to palpable mischief, will seldom fail in producing, in the end, the most serious evils, both to those who govern and those who obey."

—Samuel Miller, Ecclesiastical Tyranny from *The Ruling Elder*

American society today can be classified as a culture enamored with celebrities. Unfortunately, American Evangelicalism has followed in the footsteps of secular society. Evangelical Christians have left our first love, exchanging our Lord Jesus Christ for a mess of pottage. Evangelicalism has become a sort of spectator sport where laypeople survey the landscape to see which pastors will emerge from obscurity to obtain celebrity status. Those who obtain this position become part of a small, loyal band of brothers who are richly rewarded with prime-time speaking slots at all the big-time conferences, lucrative book contracts, and legions of fans who idolize them—attending what seems to be their monthly conferences and tweeting out their pithy nuggets to the less fortunate fans not able to attend because they couldn't afford the price of admission.

This Evangelical Industrial Complex has provided us with an incessant stream of books of questionable worth; gems such as *Crazy Busy* by Kevin DeYoung and *Real Marriage* by Mark Driscoll.

Over the years, several of the celebrity Christians have been taken down by scandals. While one would think their fellow celebrity conference speakers would be the first to call for them to step down from the stage, such has not been the case. As long as the celebrity can continue to draw fans to these venues, there will be a prime-time speaking slot reserved for him.

A recent example of this is C.J. Mahaney. Sovereign Grace Ministries, of which Mahaney was the chairman of the board and president, was embroiled in a sexual abuse scandal. Mahaney himself was credibly charged with conspiracy to cover up the abuse and the blackmail of the cofounder of the denomination, yet his fellow T4G (Together for the Gospel) celebrity speakers signed an outrageous statement of support for him. Additionally, Tim Challies, made famous by live-blogging from conferences, in his best imitation of the Wizard of Oz, "Pay no attention to the man behind the curtain," wrote an article titled "Thinking Biblically About C.J. Mahaney and Sovereign Grace Ministries." In this article, Challies stated, "I think I do well to learn less rather than more, I need to know only enough to understand that I don't need to know anything more!"

This Christian celebrity status afforded to these conference speakers has naturally infiltrated many local churches. The largely lethargic laypeople have, in many cases, ceded total control of church affairs to the senior pastor, sometimes with disastrous results, as heavy-handed authoritarian men run roughshod over compliant elder boards and the congregation.

It is in response to this abuse of authority that Robert Dixon has authored *The Uriah Syndrome*. I am greatly encouraged by Dixon's book. First, it is impressive that a layman has undertaken the massive effort needed to tackle this project and see it through to completion, and Dixon has done a masterful job. Second, it is a sign that the Holy Spirit is moving among his Body. I have detected what I believe is only the beginnings of a resurgence among the laity to return to Biblical Christianity. Almost imperceptible at first, I am seeing many who have been spiritually abused by authoritarian leadership and disenchanted with what has been going on in the Evangelical Church feel burdened enough to begin a determined effort to work for reform. Dixon's book is a helpful roadmap in this effort. Finding himself on the front lines of battle against an authoritarian pastor in a denomination that allowed no input from laypeople, Dixon worked through his discouragement, and as a result of much prayer and searching the Scripture has come to the conclusion that the root cause of spiritual abuse is *the misuse and abuse of authority*. Focusing on the priesthood of the believer and the authority of the church, Dixon challenges the laity of the church not to lose heart nor succumb to apathy, but instead "wake up and acknowledge that there is a systemic problem afoot, which can only be diverted and remedied if congregations accept responsibility to behave like the body of Christ."

To that end, I pray that, if you number yourself among the abused and disenchanted, you will draw inspiration from this book and commit to reengage in the battle. If we all work to combat heavy-handed authoritarian individuals in the church, in whatever way the Lord leads, we will help return the church to being "the light of the world," "a city set on a hill" that "cannot be hidden." (Matthew 5:14)

—Todd Wilhelm, author of the blog "Thou Art the Man"
*www.thouarttheman.org*

# ENTITIES FREQUENTLY REFERENCED IN THIS BOOK

*Sovereign Grace Ministries* first began in the 1970s as Gathering of Believers, then became known as People of Destiny, which grew to People of Destiny International, then changed names to Sovereign Grace Ministries. It was recently renamed Sovereign Grace Churches in 2014. For the purposes of this book, all references to either Sovereign Grace Ministries or Sovereign Grace Churches will be denoted by *SGM*.

At one time, SGM had over 120 churches. However, after numerous allegations of heavy-handedness, the dismissal of more than one hundred pastors, and various allegations, including blackmail and the cover-up of child sexual abuse with mitigation and legal fees costing hundreds of thousands of dollars, thousands of members left, leaving SGM half of its original size.

The SGM movement was founded and led by Larry Tomczak and C. J. Mahaney. Tomczak later left the movement in the late 1990s, after allegedly being blackmailed by Mahaney.[1] Since that time, SGM has been primarily led by Mahaney until controversy began regarding the allegations of blackmail and the cover-up of sexual abuse, particularly in the church Mahaney

---

[1] "Larry Tomczak's Story," SGM Survivors, December 2, 2011, https://www.sgmsurvivors.com/2011/12/02/larry-tomczaks-story/.

founded, Covenant Life Church (CLC) in Gaithersburg, Maryland. Several lawsuits were filed regarding the alleged cover-up of sexual abuse, but they were eventually dismissed due to legal technicalities (and not the merits of the case).[2]

Despite numerous questions, concerns, and appeals by CLC members, Mahaney abruptly left his congregation, which he had referred to in sermons as "the happiest place on earth," and moved the SGM headquarters to Louisville, Kentucky, where he is now lead pastor of Sovereign Grace Church of Louisville. Despite Mahaney's relocation, Rachael Denhollander, who helped expose the horrific sexual assault of at least 156 young women by physician Larry Nassar, has challenged the entire Sovereign Grace Church organization to submit itself to a fair and independent investigation regarding multiple allegations of sexual abuse cover-ups.[3]

*KingsWay Community Church* began in 1989 as Southside Church of Richmond. Located in Midlothian, Virginia, it is currently a member church of Sovereign Grace Churches. KingsWay was founded by former pastor Gene Emerson. This is the church my family and I were members of from its founding until 2012 and where I spent countless hours during the last ten years of my membership (2002–2012), challenging numerous cases of legalism, manipulation, coercion, and spiritual abuse that culminated in a churchwide meeting in 2012,

---

[2] For more information on the SGM lawsuit, visit http://www.sgmsurvivors.com/lawsuit-info/, and to read stories of the survivors, visit http://www.sgm-survivors.com/the-stories/.

[3] Mark Galli, "We Need an Independent Investigation of Sovereign Grace Ministries" (March 22, 2018), *Christianity Today*, https://www.christianitytoday.com/ct/2018/march-web-only/sovereign-grace-need-investigation-sgm-mahaney-denhollander.html.

during which the majority of members voiced their concern to the leaders regarding such behavior. Subsequently, many long-time members left the church. I decided to stay longer because I was particularly concerned with one of the most horrendous examples of spiritual abuse I've ever encountered, which is told by the victim's wife in chapter 3 of this book.

Ultimately, despite many appeals to the pastors of the church at that time, no resolution was ever realized. After spending tens of thousands of dollars of the church's money in mitigation fees over the course of several years, KingsWay Community Church eventually imploded, losing approximately 75 percent of its members. The senior pastor at that time was arrested on May 22, 2013, for the solicitation of a prostitute in Chesterfield County.[4] Like his mentor C. J. Mahaney, he did not feel compelled to resolve the serious allegations against him in a biblical manner but instead left the church he founded and eventually relocated to a different town in early 2017.[5]

*SGM Survivors* is a website started by bloggers "Kris" and "Guy" after many SGM members began coming forward regarding spiritual abuse suffered at the hands of authoritarian and abusive leaders in SGM. For more than a decade, SGM Survivors has provided an anonymous and safe haven for those traumatized by the abuse and atrocities of SGM leaders. SGM Survivors provides a forum for people to tell their stories; find compassionate support, prayer, and counsel; and otherwise process sometimes horrific abuse. Often, the posts are emo-

---

[4] Ben Orcutt, "Midlo Pastor Found Guilty of Soliciting Prostitution," *Chesterfield Observer* (Chesterfield County, VA), August 26, 2015.
[5] Further legal documents and details of this case can be found at www.sgmsurvivors.com.

tionally raw and difficult to read. Some of the stories and legal documents are uncomfortably explicit regarding alleged sexual abuse. Parental discretion is advised.

Sadly, allegations of sexual, physical, emotional, and spiritual abuse continue to occur in other denominations, congregations, and organizations throughout the world, bringing scathing reproach against the name of Christ and His people. Websites like SGM Survivors have appeared across the internet in an effort to provide a place where those harmed by abusive leaders and churches can document, process, counsel, and pray with others affected by this pernicious problem. In that spirit, SGM Survivors has helped countless individuals throughout the world process abuse and begin the road to recovery. Another website, which is no longer online but contributed immensely to the care of those reeling from the effects of SGM, was SGM Refuge, founded by "Jim."

I, along with many of my brothers and sisters in Christ, want to thank "Kris," "Guy," and "Jim" for providing a vital ministry to thousands of people who have been disillusioned and traumatized by abusive church leaders and enabling congregations. Thank you for your patience, endurance, and insightful commentary—and especially for your continuing compassion and love for the saints.

For more information on SGM and other topics discussed in this book, please visit the following sites:

www.sgmsurvivors.com
www.thouarttheman.org
www.wartburgwatch.com
www.brentdetwiler.com
www.netgrace.org
https://www.facebook.com/OfficialDenhollander/

# Introduction

This book is my effort to provoke thoughtful consideration regarding the root cause of spiritual abuse—namely, the *misuse and abuse of authority*—and to consider some of its most debilitating implications. To those affected by spiritual abuse, I pray this material proves helpful and encouraging and that it ministers hope, healing, and a way forward. To those unfamiliar with spiritual abuse, I pray that by considering the content herein, you may never have to experience such a pernicious but avoidable problem.

The stories in this book are actual accounts of brothers and sisters in the body of Christ, many of whom my wife and I have had the privilege of counseling. You may find some of their stories difficult to read and/or believe. The names of the survivors have been changed to maintain anonymity and confidentiality. When a story herein is a matter of legal and/or public record, the material is presented as reflected in court documents and/or public media. The accounts found in this book are genuine and the survivors of abuse require our continued prayer and support. The purpose of sharing these stories is to promote awareness of this very real but often ignored problem.

# My Story

In early 1982, I stepped inside a new church, thrilled to join a fellowship where the Spirit of God seemed to be at work. I had no idea I was about to embark on a decades-long emotional roller coaster in which powerful preaching and wonderful fellowship were mixed with subtle manipulation and false teaching. I was eventually shunned, ostracized, and despised by those in the congregation whom I had broken bread with for years. To make matters worse, the church regularly taught that submitting to and obeying the leadership was necessary for my spiritual health, as well as the health of the church as a whole. I now know that what I experienced was spiritual abuse, but I didn't recognize it at the time. It was often very subtle, and only a few other people seemed troubled by what was going on—especially since it was coming from the pulpit. Little did I know, it was like a Trojan horse that had snuck inside the congregation, creating dysfunction and causing tremendous harm to thousands of unsuspecting church members.

Hoping for change, I remained a member of that church, KingsWay Community Church in Richmond, Virginia, where I confronted leaders who continued to misuse and abuse their authority. Then in 2001, I had a watershed experience that caused me to recognize these abuses were not just limited to my church but, in my opinion, were destructive and systemic to the entire network of more than 120 churches of which KingsWay was a member—Sovereign Grace Ministries (SGM). At that time, a good friend of mine who was an associate pastor of KingsWay was given an ultimatum by senior leaders to move to another town in order to pastor a new church or risk the

# Contents

Acknowledgment .................................................................... 7
Foreword ................................................................................ 9
Entities Frequently Referenced in This Book ...................... 15
Introduction .......................................................................... 19
Chapter 1     A Simple Question .............................................. 29
Chapter 2     Peeling the Onion ............................................... 34
Chapter 3     Susan and Mark's Story ..................................... 39
Chapter 4     How Did We Get Here? ..................................... 49
Chapter 5     What Is Spiritual Abuse? .................................... 70
Chapter 6     The Church: Asleep at the Wheel ..................... 99
Chapter 7     Polity Is Not the Problem ................................ 115
Chapter 8     Theology Is Not the Problem ......................... 126
Chapter 9     The Authority of Leaders ................................ 144
Chapter 10    The Authority of the Church .......................... 179
Chapter 11    The Voice That Matters ................................... 213
Chapter 12    The Keys ........................................................... 232
Appendix 1    Exit Counseling from Spiritual Abuse ............ 238
Appendix 2    Scriptures Demonstrating the Authority and Activity of the Church Throughout the New Testament ........................................................ 240
Appendix 3    A Sample Letter to Your Congregation ......... 246
Appendix 4    Post-Traumatic Stress Disorder (PTSD) and Spiritual Abuse ............................ 250
References .......................................................................... 270
Bibliography ...................................................................... 272

loss of his job. As a result, he was fired, publicly shamed, and castigated. It was one of the most blatant abuses of spiritual authority I have ever witnessed. At that time, I had embraced many of SGM's false teachings, doctrines, and cultish practices, particularly regarding the authority of church leaders, so I publicly supported my friend's shaming. Like other members in the church, I had been deceived by years of dubious teaching on spiritual authority and the expectation of unquestioned obedience to church leadership.

By God's grace, I came to realize something was terribly wrong a few months afterward. At first, I couldn't put my finger on it, but as the supposed "process of restoration" for my friend played out, the gnawing pit in my stomach and unrest in my spirit only increased. It became obvious that there was no concern or love for my friend and his family, and no effort made for his restoration to the congregation. There was only ostracism, silence, and scorn. During that ordeal, the Lord graciously opened my eyes to see, for the first time, the destructive and toxic culture characterized by SGM and its churches. So after a decade of concerted efforts, appeals, and fruitless long meetings, my wife and I met with the pastor of KingsWay to explain our reasons for withdrawing our church membership. This was also our last appeal for leaders in the church to renounce and rectify the numerous atrocities exacted against my friend, my family, and many other church members.

While the conclusion of this meeting marked our final departure, it would not prove to be our last involvement with the SGM organization. My wife and I began to help and counsel others who had been adversely affected by the toxic culture of SGM churches. Prior to our exit, we had witnessed KingsWay grow to approximately seven hundred members, but in less than one year after our meeting with the pastor, membership was less than two hundred people. Hundreds of longtime members left because they received no response in their attempts to address problems that were evident to many people in the church. A current member recently told me, "It's not like it used to be. There's like a cloud of depression hanging over the church. There's a real sadness. But we continue to pray for God's blessing."

This is a common perspective of people who choose to remain in dysfunctional churches—they fail to recognize a simple biblical principle: God's blessing on a church must be preceded by the genuine repentance of leaders and church members toward those they have wronged (Acts 3:19–20). Sadly, this prerequisite is rarely embraced. Most remaining members and leaders persist in believing they have done nothing wrong. They do not recognize the problems that are obvious to so many. Therefore, like other churches that have made similar errors in judgement, they will one day likely close their doors.

I tell my story because I want others to know I have been on both sides of the misuse and abuse of authority. I have been guilty of misusing and abusing spiritual authority over others, and I've been sorely hurt by spiritual abuse propagated toward myself, my family, and my fellow believers. My wife and I have had the privilege of counseling and helping others exit from destructive churches and process the trauma of their experiences. We have wept and agonized with many of our brothers and sisters in Christ. We have attended the memorial service of one family who lost their child to suicide that was directly related to abusive leadership practices, and we know of others who have experienced the same tragedy with family members and friends. We've sat with brokenhearted wives and husbands, whose spouses chose loyalty to a cultlike organization rather than to their spouse. We have seen countless young people reject God and voice increasing disdain and disillusionment toward God and/or any form of organized church. We've witnessed churches of all sizes dissolve completely when members left because their leaders refused to humble themselves and listen to those they claimed to care for and pastor.

What I learned through my experience was that two primary factors contribute to dysfunctional, abusive churches: (1) authoritarian, controlling leaders and (2) passive congregations who, by their silence, enable those leaders to continue their abuse and control. In this book, I focus on the error and culpability of both, and I offer a biblical solution to the problem.

Make no mistake, I am a strong advocate for biblical leadership that's informed and constrained by Scripture. I support *servant* leadership characterized by Christ as taught in Mark 10:42–45, which places primary emphasis on *serving*. Congregations are sure to thrive where such leadership is demonstrated, and church members would do well to promote and support this type of leadership in their congregations. However, when leadership functions without recognizing the boundaries and constraints placed upon them by Scripture, the misuse and abuse of their authority is inevitable. Perhaps most lacking in the church today are humble, passionate, courageous leaders who demonstrate respect and deference toward the congregations they lead. Sadly, leaders of this caliber remain unrecognized primarily because many churches fail to exercise their biblical responsibility to choose and put forward *from among their own congregations* such individuals the congregants see fit to serve in this capacity (Acts 1:23, 6:3–6). Instead, churches will often allow other leaders from outside the membership of their own church to select individuals for leadership positions—divorced from the consideration or will of the congregation.

If a church does not have spiritually strong and robust members who are confident and secure in their own biblical responsibility and authority to choose their own leaders, it's unlikely that church will enjoy the benefits of benevolent leadership. Moreover, leaders who insist on their congregations embracing a top-down, authoritarian style of leadership will often endure church splits—even the loss of their entire congregation—rather than bow their knee to the prospect of losing control and authority over those they claim to care for. Meanwhile, church members remain passive, even though they have a biblical responsibility and authority[6] to stop abusive leaders. Therefore, they become complicit in their own demise. The aims of this book are (1) to appeal for reform where the misuse and abuse of authority in the church exists, (2) to discuss key components and misconceptions regarding biblical authority, and (3) to offer biblical solutions that promote spiritual health in the life of the individual believer, as well as the entire church.

Some authors I cite in this book have publicly supported pastors whom many Christians perceive to be spiritually abusive. But while I am grieved by the statements and actions of some of my favorite and most influential authors and pastors, I *will* reference them in this book when what they have to say is helpful and supported by Scripture. Jesus said to "practice and observe whatever [the Pharisees] tell you—but not what they do. For they preach, but do not practice" (Mathew 23:3). Jesus

---

[6] See chapter 10, "The Authority of the Church."

commended the *knowledge* of the Pharisees but disagreed with their *application* of that knowledge. Likewise, I choose to "chew the meat and spit out the bones," as my father used to say, and I hope you can too.

Finally, I am deeply indebted to those who have gone before me in exposing and providing insight regarding spiritual abuse. Those books holding particular influence in my life include *Churches That Abuse* by Ron Enroth, *Counseling Survivors of Sexual Abuse* by Diane Langberg, *Healing Spiritual Abuse* by Ken Blue, *Hurt People Hurt People* by Sandra Wilson, *Recovering from Churches That Abuse* by Ron Enroth, and *The Subtle Power of Spiritual Abuse* by David Johnson and Jeff VanVonderen. These and many other helpful reference materials are listed in the back of this book. I'm also grateful for the work of Steven Hassan, who, with the help of family and friends, was extricated from the Moonies in 1976 and has subsequently been helping others worldwide to free themselves from abusive and cultlike organizations.

While the pioneering work of these authors laid the foundation of how to understand spiritual abuse, I found myself at a loss to identify with reasonable confidence its root cause. As I examined the problem and "peeled the onion"—something we say in the counseling community—I discovered at the core the simple idea that *spiritual abuse is directly related to the misunderstanding and misapplication of authority*. A well-known biblical story helps illustrate this point: the story of David and Bathsheba in 2 Samuel 11. Let's turn there now.

## The Uriah Syndrome

*Why have you despised the word of the LORD, to do what is evil in his sight? You have struck down Uriah the Hittite with the sword and have taken his wife to be your wife and have killed him with the sword of the Ammonites.*

—2 Samuel 12:9 (ESV)

The story of David and Bathsheba begins in wartime when David, the king, has sent his soldiers out to battle while he himself stays home. One evening, he notices from his palace roof a beautiful young woman bathing, and he lusts after her. He finds out her name, Bathsheba, and that she is married to Uriah, one of David's soldiers who is away at war. But instead of averting his eyes from her and subduing his passions, he exercises his authority and power as king and sends for her. When she arrives, David fulfills his desires and sleeps with her, conceiving a child. When Bathsheba discovers she's pregnant, she tells David, who devises an insidious plan. He calls Uriah back from battle and urges him to go home and relax, hoping he will sleep with Bathsheba. But Uriah, remaining loyal to his king, chooses to sleep at the door of the palace instead of with his wife. David tries a second time to get Uriah to sleep with Bathsheba by getting him drunk, but Uriah steadfastly remains at the palace. Twice, Uriah ends up thwarting David's attempts simply by being a faithful and loyal servant.

Frustrated, David sends Uriah back to war and tells the commander of the army to purposely place Uriah on the front lines of battle and then draw back from him so he would be struck down and killed. David makes no effort to hide his evil intentions, knowing that the commander is also a faithful servant and will remain loyal even at the expense of one of his comrades. The plan succeeds: Uriah is abandoned at the front lines and subsequently killed by the enemy. When Bathsheba hears her husband is dead, she weeps and mourns for him. After her grief ends, David marries her, and she gives birth to a son. But what David did displeased the Lord, and there would be serious consequences for his actions.

I find this story to be a sad but fitting analogy in which a leader wields his power and authority to take advantage of loyal, faithful people in order to advance his own agenda. In this illustration, David represents church leaders who misuse and abuse their authority. Like David, these leaders typically want to advance their own agendas and satisfy their desire to maintain power, control, and authority over God's people. Similar to David, they will typically stop at nothing to obtain this end—even to the point of losing an entire church.

Uriah, in contrast, represents the members of the church hurt by these selfish and controlling leaders. Like most members in a local church, Uriah is faithful, loyal, and obedient. He always believes the best of his king, even when his king acts in ways that should raise suspicion.

In the end, David's lust for something God has not permitted him to have ends up in disaster for everyone. Uriah is killed; Bathsheba loses her husband; and David's son, the fruit of his evil deed, dies soon after he is born.

David was a leader who misused and abused his authority for selfish gain, even at the cost of harming the very people he was called to care for and protect—even while they maintained unquestioned loyalty and faithfulness, regardless of what they were asked to do or believe.

Similarly, such a scenario leaves in its wake vast numbers of God's people who feel stranded, deserted, and disillusioned by those entrusted to care for them as a shepherd does his sheep. Many times, these congregants are shunned by their own family and other members of their church at the instruction of misguided and abusive leaders, insisting that those who raise any concerns regarding leadership are rebellious and divisive. Additionally, the dysfunction and harm produced by such malfeasance usually manifests a wide array of symptoms like anger, resentment, cynicism, grief, depression, anxiety, acute stress, paranoia, flashbacks, panic attacks, nightmares, and an aversion to certain persons, places, or situations (especially related to God and/or church).

For these reasons, I don't think the term *spiritual abuse* adequately captures the complexities and trauma associated with the misuse and abuse of authority in the church. However, since *spiritual abuse* is still normative nomenclature in the literature, I will continue to use that terminology throughout this book to refer to what I otherwise personally call—the *Uriah syndrome*.[7]

---

[7] A *syndrome* is a co-occurring set of signs and symptoms that corporately characterize a particular dysfunction.

# 1

# A Simple Question

*Behold, the* L<small>ORD</small> passed by, and a great and strong wind tore the mountains and broke in pieces the rocks before the L<small>ORD</small>, *but the* L<small>ORD</small> *was not in the wind. And after the wind an earthquake, but the* L<small>ORD</small> was not in the earthquake. And after the earthquake a fire, but the L<small>ORD</small> *was not in the fire. And after the fire the sound of a low whisper.*

—1 Kings 19:11–12

I sank down in the couch with my head in my hands. Disgust gave way to fear as I contemplated the chain of events during the past few months. Several of us in the church had just made what appeared to be the final appeal to our leaders, urging them to reconsider their decision to publicly disgrace and discipline a beloved pastor. To make matters worse, many other atrocities were exposed in the course of our appeals, which our leaders denied and minimized despite overwhelming evidence.

We had no idea where we could find an appropriate forum to hold these men accountable for their callous behavior. After all, it was *their* job to handle these kinds of things—wasn't it?

Our church had always been taught that leaders had a special anointing the rest of us laypeople did not possess. But now they were causing harm! What were we supposed to do?

A wave of discouragement and frustration washed over me as I realized that despite our best efforts, the men responsible for the devastation and destruction of our brother would be adjudicating their *own* despicable behavior! The senior pastor who had led the charge was going to be held accountable by three of his own loyal colleagues. How could they possibly be impartial judges? Their paychecks were even signed by the same man they were supposed to impartially judge! The absurdity was laughable.

Something felt very, very wrong, but I couldn't put my finger on it. How could our church have found itself in this situation? Wasn't it supposed to be "the pillar and foundation of the truth"? More questions clouded my mind. Did the Bible really teach and expect a congregation to give leaders such unconditional loyalty, submission, and obedience simply *because* they were leaders? Was there no biblical recourse in difficult situations like the one we now faced? Were laypeople like me just supposed to "know our place" and trust our leaders to take care of things since they were "keeping watching over our souls"? At least that's what we were taught from Hebrews 13:17. Were we really supposed to unconditionally obey our leaders "with joy and not with groaning," even in the face of gross misconduct and bad teaching? Was a church supposed to remain passive and impotent, paralyzed by blind obedience, while its leaders' sins suffocated the congregation?

Another wave of despair washed away any remaining hope I might have had. "What am I to do!" I cried to the Lord. "What are *we* to do as a church?"

And then, as if carried by a gentle breeze from heaven, the still, small voice of God pierced my troubles with a single question: *Does the church have authority?*

Instantly, hope flushed through me. I had never even considered this simple question.

Over the next year, this new concept profoundly changed my life. It seemed like every waking moment, I was turning the question over in my mind. As I dug into the Word with renewed zeal, I found myself refreshed with hope and emboldened in faith as each new nugget of truth began to shape new convictions in me. In my excitement, I often found myself preaching mini-sermons to my wife and children on the wonder, brilliance, and beauty of the *authority of the church* that permeated the New Testament. This simple truth fundamentally changed our lives—first as individual believers, then later as members of the body of Christ. Indeed, it began to liberate our souls and provide hope and direction as we navigated the difficult but exciting waters ahead. For the first time in our Christian lives, we envisioned a strong, robust, and participatory church as reflected throughout the New Testament. With new eyes, we began to see God's people embrace their responsibility to choose leaders, be centrally involved in making weighty decisions and judgments, provide input on finances, and to send and receive leaders as they ministered among other New Testament congregations.

As we studied the Scriptures, it felt like we were beholding the majesty of the church for the first time. The new paradigm we were starting to embrace was completely contrary to that which was taught by our former leaders. They had had a vested interest to maintain authority over the congregation at any cost, so they continually preached sermons designed to convince our church to unconditionally obey and submit to them. They said they had a "special anointing" and greater spiritual aptitude, so they were always emphasizing our obligation to remain subservient to them, the elite few, who were "over us in the Lord."

Little by little, the ominous and foreboding stronghold of thoughts, ideas, and teachings we had believed and practiced for years began to crumble in front of us. Like Saul, the scales fell from our eyes as we enthusiastically studied God's Word, filling us with hope and joy as we began to see clearly the majesty, glory, awesome responsibility, and authority given to God's people. With newfound insight and direction, we slowly disentangled ourselves from a cultic expression of Christianity and began to experience freedom and healing as a family by denouncing and repenting of the toxic church culture and value system that had plagued our lives for so long. As our knowledge and understanding of what it meant to be a responsible church member steadily grew, we realized that God, through His Word, had indeed answered the surprising question He had whispered to me during one of the most troubling times of my Christian life. The story of that answer and how it profoundly changed our lives is in the pages that follow.

# Study Notes

# 2

# Peeling the Onion

*Now these Jews were more noble than those in Thessalonica; they received the word with all eagerness, examining the Scriptures daily to see if these things were so.*

—Acts 17:11

*As we bring our stories into the light...falsehoods, darkness, and deception are more likely to be exposed; the scales are loosened...better to see. Chains are broken...and captives set free.*

—"Mole," SGM Survivors

These are sobering times for Christians in America. Every day, more news stories appear that reveal various types of abuse in the church. How can Christians respond? What is the solution? What causes such serious maladies in the church today? As a professional counselor, I have thought deeply about these questions and, after spending many hours in prayer and searching the Scriptures for answers, believe I have something to offer.

In counseling, a clinician applies a diagnostic principle whenever he assesses a patient—he makes a concerted effort to eliminate competing diagnoses in his attempt to arrive at the correct diagnosis. He does this in order to distinguish a particular condition from others that present similar clinical features. For example, if a patient presents with anxiety, restlessness, and difficulty focusing, the clinician may seek to rule out attention deficit hyperactivity disorder (ADHD) or find out if there have been any medication changes or illicit drug use. He may want to inquire about paranoia or whether or not there are hallucinations accompanying the anxiety. Is the anxiety chronic and pervasive, or is it sporadic and triggered by specific stressors? Has the individual experienced any unusual trauma like war, aggravated assault, or abuse?

These are the types of questions that help a clinician arrive at an accurate diagnosis, increasing the probability of implementing an appropriate intervention. Ultimately, it makes a huge difference if the individual has general anxiety verses bipolar disorder with psychotic features or PTSD.

Likewise, when considering the etiology or root cause of spiritual abuse, it behooves us as Christians to apply a similar process and ask questions in our attempt to arrive at an accurate principle diagnosis since a proper diagnosis is a prerequisite for determining the most effective interventions. In counseling, this process of inquiry, vetting, and ruling out peripheral factors continues in subsequent sessions where therapists use their professional expertise, as well as various assessment tools, to "peel the onion," as we say, and eventually discover the core or essence of the problem.

When I counsel individuals who have been spiritually abused, I ask them, "How do you think spiritual abuse occurs?

Where does it come from? What factors do you think contribute to it?"

In response, I tend to get a broad range of answers:

"Abusive leaders."

"Leaders with 'type A' personalities."

"Heavy-handed leaders."

"Narcissistic leaders."

"Leaders who believe they have a superior and special anointing."

"A top-down model of leadership."

"Oppressive church government structures."

One of the most surprising answers has been, "The Bible says we have to submit to and obey our leaders—but sometimes, they have control issues!" Others give more academic answers: "*Church polity* is the root of the problem," or "One's *theological understanding of leadership* is the problem."

So which is it? What's the real cause of spiritual abuse? *Is there even a root cause?* Are we destined to settle for ambiguity and frustration on a vexing issue that continues to gather disturbing momentum throughout the church? Can we realistically expect to arrive at an accurate diagnosis?

I believe we can.

I think we can discover a clear diagnosis of the root cause of spiritual abuse, and we can implement appropriate interventions regarding this pernicious scourge—but only if we are willing to do the hard work of ruling out other possible culprits. We must be willing to dig deep in order to discover the core issue. We must be determined and diligent in our study of Scripture, just like the Bereans in Acts 17:11, who "received the word with all eagerness, examining the Scriptures daily to see if these things were so."

Likewise, though our eyes may sting with tears and a pungent odor burns our nostrils, we must be willing to peel the onion of spiritual abuse. So brace yourself for the task at hand. We will begin by looking at one of the most profound cases of spiritual abuse I have ever witnessed.

# Study Notes

many people came up to Mark suggesting that Roanoke was *his* opportunity to lay his life down—just like Paul in Jerusalem. I was excited. Mark felt pressured. Since the Roanoke group had come to the conference, Mark was asked to meet with them with them and share that we were seriously considering taking the leadership role.

At 4:00 a.m., Mark suddenly woke up with a startle. We were confused, but we chalked his behavior up to being exhausted. Little did we know, this was the first of many times this would occur.

After we got home from the conference, the pressure of the whole situation lessened, and things got back to being fairly normal, so we began visiting the Roanoke folks on the weekends. Sadly, Mark had a hard time bonding with the church there, which surprised me, since he loved the mountainous area and seemed to have so much compassion for the group.

It raised a question in my heart, but I didn't have much room for it. Roanoke was supposed to be our Jerusalem, right?

When August came around, the pressure of the Roanoke situation was weighing heavily on Mark. He knew that everyone was waiting on a decision, and he was dragging his feet with an answer. He couldn't eat and was barely sleeping. During this time, Mark met with a friend who spoke of a similar time in his own life where he wasn't eating or sleeping right and that he too had felt the kind of panic that Mark felt. For him, the cause was *unbelief*.

Unbelief! *That was our problem*, we thought. *Mark just wasn't trusting God!* Mark quickly went on a serious rampage to kill, crush, and destroy all unbelief in his life, and I never saw a man work more seriously in putting his flesh to death. But the more he prayed and fought, the worse his symptoms became. Mark would barely eat, so he began to lose weight, and he slept so little that he would fall asleep sitting upright. *Soon*, we thought, God will have victory, and the ugly monster of unbelief will die! We were both very hard on ourselves during this time, and we questioned every motive and thought of our own hearts to the point where it was impossible to find anything good coming from our "wicked hearts"!

As Mark continued to wrestle with the decision to take the leadership role at Roanoke, he decided he needed a personal retreat, so he left for a couple days to pray. On the way home, he called me, saying, "Hon, the heavens were brass—I never got a sense that God was saying anything!" I was so discouraged.

Shortly afterward, Mark and I went to another retreat. This time, it was for the pastors of churches in our region, along with their wives. We told them about our entire journey thus far, and Mark shared with them a list of pros and cons he had created to help make a decision. The list was light on the pros and heavy on the cons, and when he read it aloud, everyone decided that his reasons for staying in Richmond were selfish. I felt conflicted since I had not seen selfishness in my husband since the earliest years of our marriage! Still, we continued to convince Mark of his "error"; and by the end of that retreat, Mark believed he was being ruled in his heart by both *selfishness* and *wicked unbelief*.

We finally decided to take a vacation in order to make a final decision about what to do, and we met with the SGM regional leader for lunch. He was considered by all of SGM to be an apostle, and his opinions held serious spiritual weight. While we ate, he told us that Mark would not have a job in Richmond if he refused to go to Roanoke. I felt ill, swallowed my food hard, and attempted a smile.

A few days later, I called him again and told him that "it was all over" and that we were leaving Roanoke. I feared for my husband's life and led him away from the city by the hand. It was the saddest day of my life.

Just prior to moving, we made a trip to Raleigh, North Carolina, out of desperation and met with a couple we were very close with who lovingly took the time to listen to our saga. When they heard the full story, they were extremely concerned about the way things were handled. Ugh! I wished we had made them aware of the whole story before now! They spent the next forty-eight hours caring for us, listening to us, and crying with us.

As we headed back to Roanoke to begin packing for our return to Richmond, our regional leader flew into town and requested to meet with us. We accepted, and during our meeting, he told us that Mark was not too far off from becoming like Nebuchadnezzar (whom God made insane due to disobedience) and that it was a good thing Mark wasn't "eating grass" yet.

I cried inside. It was one of the most cruel, uncompassionate statements I have ever heard out of the mouth of a pastor. I've never gotten over those painful words. Then to make matters worse, the regional leader forbade us from ever changing our story. He told us, "There will never be any revisionist history." To make matters even worse, our senior pastor demanded that we write a letter addressed to every pastor in the entire SGM network stating that the reason Mark was stepping down from ministry was because of his selfishness and the "sin of wicked unbelief."

At this point, we decided to visit the Christian Counseling and Education Foundation in Philadelphia. Our counselor there expressed significant concerns about Mark's relationship with our former senior pastor and how things were handled. After a few sessions of counseling, that former senior pastor recommended that we end our counseling and instead be cared for by another couple of his choosing. We went along with it. They attempted to care for us, but the discussions never went anywhere because we couldn't share the whole truth with them.

As we were preparing to return to Richmond, the churches in both Richmond and Roanoke held meetings to communicate Mark's sins of selfishness and unbelief. We were present at the meeting in Roanoke, and I agonized through the whole thing. A few loving women wrapped their arms around me, but I couldn't tell them that everything they were hearing was wrong. I could only cry. Each church then preached on the wickedness and repercussions of unbelief for an entire month. Though Mark's name was never mentioned, it didn't need to be.

When we returned to Richmond, our old church gave us a cool reception. People were told not to get involved with us. Those whom we considered our friends were not sure what to do. Many kept their distance, and many of those once-close relationships are still not the same to this day. In the end, though we lost our home, our employment, and our dignity, what hurt the most was losing the affection and trust of our spiritual family.

We still couldn't share the truth of what happened. For so long, we could only carry it inside of us. When I prayed with other ladies, I couldn't reveal the real thing I needed prayer for. I couldn't joyfully greet the leaders because I couldn't be honest with them. Mark sometimes attempted to revisit the issue with the regional leader, but the regional leader maintained that there was no wrong done and reiterated that everything was due only to my husband's sin.

I know that I myself did not help the situation by putting undue pressure on Mark, and I have asked him to forgive me multiple times. My biggest prayer is that our church would likewise repent and grow in stature as the wrongs against my husband are made right. I think that it would benefit the entire church to hear that there was more to our story than what they heard. My prayer is that Mark would be fully restored and even applauded as a man of faith, loyalty, and perseverance under trial. Sadly, I do not think that now my husband can ever be truly restored. The effects from this season wreaked havoc on his mind. He now suffers with extreme torment day and night but continues to encourage me and others as he prays for those in need late into the night. He has become one of the forgotten, but not by God. Other than Jesus, my husband, Mark, is my biggest hero. This is our story.

*****

*Nine years later, after a psychiatric hospitalization and more than thirty electroconvulsive treatments, Mark is unable to hold down a job and is now on full disability due to chronic and severe depression. He wakes up to debilitating panic attacks which last a good part of the morning, then sits in a chair in a dark room and watches sports on television for the remainder of the day. He very seldom leaves the room, and a regimen of pills help him sleep at night. Not many people visit him. As the years pass, he appears to have been forgotten.*

# Study Notes

# 4

# How Did We Get Here?

*Not that we lord it over your faith, but we work with you for your joy, for you stand firm in your faith.*
—2 Corinthians 1:24

*Whereas Christians are encouraged to support and submit to spiritual leadership (Hebrews 13:17), such encouragement must not be considered a blank check if churches are responsible for and have the authority to discipline false teachers and to recognize an antecedent commitment not to a pastor but to the truth of the Gospel.*[8]
—D.A. Carson, Church Authority

The Jesus Movement of the late 1960s and early '70s was an exciting time as a mighty outpouring of the Spirit swept tens of thousands of young men and women into the church. Massive throngs of people were saved at Jesus festivals and outdoor concerts. Street preachers could barely extend invitations for

---

[8] D.A. Carson, "Authority in the Church," in *Evangelical Dictionary of Theology*, ed. Walter Elwell (Grand Rapids: Baker, 2001), 251.

salvation before those listening would repent and confess Christ as their Savior.[9]

Many churches exploded with growth as people came to know the Lord. But the waves of revival receded during the mid-1970s, leaving in their wake a mixture of both healthy, robust churches and unhealthy, aberrant churches. Several authoritarian church groups sprouted in cities and rural areas throughout the country, like the Children of God, the Church of Bible Understanding, and the Twelve Tribes. These groups were usually led by charismatic but legalistic and demanding leaders who touted the latest alleged revelation of God, which appealed to people who were searching and longing to know more of the Lord.

During this time, a group gained traction that later became known as the Shepherding Movement. Led by Bob Mumford, Ern Baxter, Don Basham, Derek Prince, and Charles Simpson (commonly known as the Fab Five), the group probably began as a relatively healthy expression of the body of Christ, but it soon manifested an authoritarian leadership style that ultimately wreaked havoc in the lives of many of its followers. According to the Shepherding Movement, the idea of being "discipled" and having a "spiritual covering" was necessary to mature in one's relationship with Christ. These terms and ideas may sound innocuous, but in the Shepherding Movement, they ensured that leaders exercised unquestioned authority in virtually every aspect of life of those who were being "discipled."

Where to live, whom to date, whom to marry, how to spend money, how to raise and educate children—these were

---

[9] Pictures, music, key people, and a chronological historical account of this very special time can be found online at http://one-way.org/jesusmovement/.

fought "unbelief" in every spare minute he was awake. Our former senior pastor eventually allowed Mark to take medication, so we visited a doctor who immediately put Mark on Paxil. His symptoms didn't change. Mark was now convinced that only God could make him well. At this point, Mark was no longer capable of thinking rationally, and when I looked into his eyes, I got a blank stare. He was no longer there.

I felt very, very alone.

At this point, God brought Lance into our lives. Lance was very familiar with mortifying sin, but he'd also been hospitalized for clinical depression more than once. His church family had loved and cared for him through each and every mental episode he'd experienced, and he now did the same for Mark.

Lance quickly recognized the tell-tale symptoms of a mental illness and became an advocate for Mark. My husband *finally* had someone to talk to! The next day, I spoke with Lance's wife, Rachael, about our situation, even though I knew I was breaking the "don't tell anyone" rule. Just having someone warm and receptive who understood me brought incredible comfort! However, even with Lance and Rachael's assistance, Mark had become nearly unresponsive. Lance stressed that we had to quickly seek professional help.

I called the senior pastor in Richmond and tried to tell him about Mark's condition, but he said he was too busy to talk. I hung up. Later that week, I met with him in person and told him I was near despair and asked him what we were going to do. He said that my oldest daughter and I could get a job at Target, and if Mark ever got well enough, he could work at McDonald's. His callous words stunned me.

Over the next several weeks, Mark began to lose a significant amount of weight and continued to be unable to sleep, waking up every morning at four, stricken with panic. We still assumed these symptoms were from selfishness and unbelief, so we fought them with Scripture. We prayed, we read, we proclaimed, we memorized, we paced, and we even tried to cast out spirits. But the symptoms only got worse.

Our leaders told us that because our suffering was due to our sin, we were not to tell other people about what was happening to us, and Mark was discouraged from seeking a medical doctor. Instead, we were told that we just needed to move to Roanoke in order to prove that the "monster of unbelief" wasn't as scary as we thought it was.

As we were deciding whether or not to sell our house, Mark and I were discussing this "monster" with our senior pastor and his wife one day when our pastor suddenly said, "Mark, if you don't move to Roanoke, your job will be in jeopardy." I'll never forget that moment. My husband was seriously sick, but now we *had* to go, or he would definitely lose his employment. Both the regional leader and now our own senior pastor had made that clear.

Our going-away party ended with many tears. I first thought Mark was only sad because he was leaving those he loved, but he was crying uncontrollably. I couldn't tell anyone that he was behaving strangely. People asked me if he was getting enough to eat—I told them he was a little stressed. I was scared.

On December 1, we made the move to Roanoke only to find that the "monster of unbelief" was anything but dead. Mark had hoped that all his symptoms would disappear after the move, but they only got worse. For a month straight, he

# 3

# SUSAN AND MARK'S STORY

*The weak you have not strengthened, the sick you have not healed, the injured you have not bound up, the strayed you have not brought back, the lost you have not sought, and with force and harshness you have ruled them.*

—Ezekiel 34:4

*The following story is written from the perspective of the wife of a former pastor, beloved by his congregation, who was publicly shamed, disgraced, and unjustly dismissed by a unilateral decision from the senior leadership. If you have personally suffered spiritual abuse, you may want to skip to the next chapter.*

\* \* \* \* \*

What I am about to share with you are the memories of the most painful season of our lives. I really wish I didn't have to think about them, but I'm sharing our story with hope that it's helpful to others. I don't know if hindsight is twenty-twenty, as they say, but when your spouse is going through a profound mental trial, it's hard to think straight.

For many years, my husband, Mark, served on the pastoral staff of Southside Church of Richmond, which later became KingsWay Community Church. The job was hard with many unending hours of labor, but he loved it with a passion. He knew, without question, that he was called by God to care for this community of believers. He served in many capacities, holding administrative duties, leading worship, and pastoring late into the night and early in the morning. There was nothing in his life that he loved more, and he loved it with a deep sincerity and passion that still amazes me.

After ten years serving at Kingsway, we bought a house in the spring, and Mark was ordained as an associate minister of the Gospel one month later. Shortly afterward, he visited a small group of people three hours away in the city of Roanoke who hoped to be adopted by SGM to become a local church in our network of churches. Mark was moved with compassion for these sheep without a shepherd, and *we* wondered if he was supposed to be their leader.

I personally loved the idea. Mark was gifted and qualified for the job, and we had been at the church in Richmond a long time. I was ready for what God had in store for our future. I'd been reading of Jim Elliot, the Puritans, and other men who had given their lives for the cause of Christ, and I had been thinking of how I could die for Christ myself. This could be the opportunity. Mark, however, didn't share the same feelings. Though he clearly cared about the people at Roanoke, he never believed that God was calling *him* specifically to be their pastor.

However, that summer, after hearing a stirring message at the Celebration Conference, an annual gathering of team-related churches in SGM about laying one's life down for Christ,

all vetted by a leader who ultimately permitted or denied one's choices in these areas. If he was not obeyed, one risked being excommunicated or shunned by the leader of the church, as well as the entire congregation. It was not uncommon for someone to turn down a promotion if it meant moving to another town, particularly if that town had no "sister church" to join. It was difficult for outsiders to detect this heavy-handedness since much of the discipling was communicated with subtle innuendo and emotional manipulation in private meetings instead of with clear messages straight from the pulpit.

Dr. Steven Lambert, author of *Charismatic Captivation*, analyzes some of the theological and doctrinal tenets associated with this problematic leadership style and exposes subtle nuances of the Shepherding Movement's governmental structure and the polity typically practiced in their churches:

> [The authority structure] was a pyramid-shaped, multi-tiered organizational structure, which had at the top echelon of the pyramid (it just so happened) none other than the Fab Five themselves, who claimed (conveniently) to be in "submission" to each other, which arrangement, they purported, acted as a fail-safe "checks and balance" system to totally preclude them from falling prey to the corruptive properties of absolute power to which, historically, so many others (albeit, less spiritual than they, of course) succumbed.[10]

---

[10] Steven Lambert, *Charismatic Captivation* (Real Truth Publications, 2003), 27.

Eventually, the bad fruit of these practices exposed the Shepherding Movement as harmful and abusive, and it demonstrated how well-intentioned Christian leaders can bring disunity to the body of Christ and surreptitiously put those exposed to such teaching in bondage. It is evidence of how a perfectly biblical concept like authority can go awry. Dr. Ronald Enroth elaborates on the narcissistic and paranoid tendencies exhibited by these types of leaders. Unfortunately, this description still applies to many leaders in the church today:

> The religious autocrat takes pleasure in requiring obedience and subordination. His style of leadership can be described as narcissistic. His message is so intertwined with his own personality (and his fear of being weak) that he easily concludes that anyone who disagrees with him—who is not loyal to him—is in consort with the Adversary.[11]

By the mid-1980s, fallout from the overbearing practices wrought by the toxic culture inherent in the Shepherding Movement became increasingly visible to well-known pastors and Christian leaders outside the "shepherding" circles. Gordon MacDonald, one of the more popular authors and speakers at that time, made this observation:

> Abusive discipleship begins when someone seeks people with the conscious or uncon-

---

[11] Ronald Enroth, "The Power Abusers: When Follow-the-Leader Becomes a Dangerous Game," *Eternity Magazine*, October 1979, 23.

> scious aim not of growing or leading them, but of controlling them. Sadly, this can be—and often is—effectively done in the name of discipling. The extremity of this tendency is cultism.[12]

A decade later, residual effects of spiritually abusive practices spawned by the Shepherding Movement continued to manifest throughout many congregations in America and beyond. In their book, *Damaged Disciples*, Ron and Vicki Burks cite numerous examples of people devastated by the authoritarian teaching of the Shepherding Movement.

Even after the demise of the movement, what appeared to remain was the unbiblical belief that church leaders had authority over the volition of individual members in the church and, by extension, the entire congregation. This unbiblical dynamic continues to persist in many churches today, and the doctrine of the priesthood of all believers is, for the most part, a foreign concept. We will discuss this very important doctrine further in chapter 10.

By the late 1990s, the leaders of the Shepherding Movement had parted ways, and the group slowly began to dissipate. Two of its most influential leaders, Derek Prince and Bob Mumford, had already publicly distanced themselves from their previous harmful teachings. In 1983, Derek Prince had completely withdrawn from the group, saying, "We were guilty of the Galatian error: having begun in the Spirit, we quickly degenerated into

---

[12] Gordon MacDonald, "Disciple Abuse," *Discipleship Journal*, no. 30 (1985): 26.

the flesh."[13] In 1989, Bob Mumford also issued a "formal repentance statement to the body of Christ" and soon thereafter made a public statement: "Discipleship was wrong. I repent. I ask forgiveness."[14]

Despite these confessions, the seeds of the Shepherding Movement were already sown, particularly among aspiring young leaders in numerous evangelical communities throughout the United States and Europe. These leaders continued to practice a top-down authority structure, which emphasized unquestioned authority and control of church members. This resulted in pervasive "groupthink," the micromanagement of congregations, unconditional submission to leadership, and the shunning of church members who dared question any aspect, teaching, or behavior of the leadership. The congregation was regularly and systematically taught that leaders were accountable to other leaders but never to the congregation. To think otherwise was to invite accusations of rebellion and divisiveness from the leaders and the rest of the church. Conformity was the hallmark of the culture.

One community called Gathering of Believers had repeatedly exposed itself to the mentoring and leadership of the Shepherding Movement during the late 1970s and throughout the '80s. This group eventually birthed Sovereign Grace Ministries (SGM), founded by C. J. Mahaney and Larry Tomczak. Mahaney was senior pastor of Covenant Life Church, the founding church of SGM, until he passed the baton to Joshua Harris on September 19, 2004. Ten years later, SGM changed

---

[13] Derek Prince, *Jubilee 1995 Celebration: 50th Year in Ministry* (Charlotte, NC: Derek Prince Ministries, 1995), 9.

[14] "Mumford Repents of Discipleship Errors," *Charisma & Christian Life Magazine*, February 1990, 15–16.

their name to Sovereign Grace Churches after several class-action lawsuits were filed against the organization regarding allegations of promoting the practice of covering up sexual abuse in several of their churches. SGM denies that this was the reason for changing their name.

Earlier in 1997, Tomczak removed himself from SGM after being allegedly blackmailed by Mahaney.[15] For fourteen years, the elders and members of Covenant Life Church were unaware of these allegations until 2011. They then confronted Mahaney, who by that time had been their pastor for almost thirty years. Unfortunately, there was no resolution, and Mahaney left abruptly that same year, finding refuge at nearby Capitol Hill Baptist Church, led by Mark Dever. Mahaney later left the region altogether and moved to Louisville, Kentucky, where he began a new church in 2012, Sovereign Grace Church of Louisville.

Scandalous accusations surrounding Mahaney are extensive and continue to follow him as of the writing of this book. Several of the most notable allegations will be cited throughout the book since Mahaney is, in the opinion of many, a notorious and long-standing example of abusive authoritarian leadership. Yet he continues to be regularly defended by several nationally known evangelical leaders,[16] despite compelling evidence of harmful leadership practices, including the recent alleged cover-up of sexual abuse made public by lawyer Rachel Denhollander, who called it "one of the most well-documented

---

[15] "Larry Tomczak's Story," SGM Survivors, December 2, 2011, https://www.sgmsurvivors.com/2011/12/02/larry-tomczaks-story/.

[16] Mark Dever, Ligon Duncan, Al Mohler, "Statement," Together for the Gospel, May 23, 2013, https://web.archive.org/web/20130606205256/http://t4g.org/statement/.

cases of institutional cover-up I have ever seen."[17] Moreover, Denhollander, who spearheaded the Larry Nassar sexual abuse case, speaks of a "systematic burying of reports of sexual assault" inside the American evangelical church. She claims that out of all the insurance claims filed against churches, *evangelical* churches have the most reports of sexual abuse.[18]

*Christianity Today* also followed the story of the lawsuit filed against SGM:

> A controversial lawsuit alleging leaders of Sovereign Grace Ministries [SGM] conspired to conceal the sexual abuse of children has been amended a second time, adding three more plaintiffs and a large number of graphic claims.
>
> The amended lawsuit makes the stark claim that SGM leaders "conspired, and continue to conspire, to permit sexual deviants to have unfettered access to children for purposes of predation, and to obstruct justice by covering up ongoing and past predation." It alleges that SGM leaders failed to fulfill mandatory reporting obligations, and instead had

---

[17] Morgan Lee, "My Larry Nassar Testimony Went Viral. But There's More to the Gospel Than Forgiveness," *Christianity Today*, January 31, 2018, https://www.christianitytoday.com/ct/2018/january-web-only/rachael-denhollander-larry-nassar-forgiveness-gospel.html.

[18] Megan Briggs, "Rachael Denhollander on Fox: Evangelicals and Abuse," Church Leaders, March 29, 2018, https://churchleaders.com/news/321299-rachael-denhollander-on-fox-evangelicals-and-abuse.html.

alleged victims meet with and forgive their abusers.[19]

*Christianity Today* later reported that because the statute of limitations had expired for most of the plaintiffs in the case (and because others had filed suit in the wrong state), the original lawsuit had been dismissed,[20] regardless of its merits. At this, many Christians, particularly several prominent evangelical leaders, expressed their indignation, angst, and disappointment at the leadership of Sovereign Grace Ministries for not having taken responsibility for the alleged abuse that occurred on their watch.

Professor and theologian Scot McKnight wrote of a "blatant failure" to "recognize the complicity of a leader in what transpired under his watch." Boz Tchividjian, a longtime advocate for victims of sexual abuse, called the allegations "one of the most disturbing accounts of child sexual abuse and institutional 'cover up' I have read in my almost 20 years of addressing this issue" and that the SGM leaders "have once again, and perhaps unwittingly, demonstrated the art of marginalizing individual souls for the sake of reputation and friendships." Tchividjian also commented on the lawsuit's dismissal:

---

[19] Jeremy Weber, "Lawsuit Claiming Church Conspiracy to Conceal Child Abuse Adds More Names and Charges," *Christianity Today* online, May 13, 2014, https://www.christianitytoday.com/news/2013/may/lawsuit-claiming-church-conspiracy-to-conceal-child-abuse.html.

[20] Jeremy Weber, "C. J. Mahaney Breaks Silence on Sovereign Grace Ministries Abuse Allegations," *Christianity Today* online, May 22, 2014, https://www.christianitytoday.com/news/2014/may/c-j-mahaney-breaks-silence-sovereign-grace-ministries-sgm.html.

> Does this mean that a jury is required in order to determine the existence of evil? .... Such an approach to sin is incredibly damaging to so many precious individuals who were sexually victimized for years and manipulated by perpetrators and church leaders into remaining silent. It tells them that their voice and experience doesn't matter nearly as much as the voice of a judge or jury.[21]

Another recent example of the destructive nature of heavy-handed, authoritarian leadership likely influenced by the abusive culture of the Shepherding Movement is the case of Mark Driscoll, a megachurch pastor formerly based in Seattle, Washington. Driscoll began his ministry in 1996 at the age of twenty-five, and his congregation at Mars Hill Church eventually grew to more than twelve thousand people with fifteen satellite locations in five states. He was well-known for his bombastic preaching style and frequent allusions to sexual topics. Many people felt his habit of being very explicit with his language was crass and unnerving. He is perhaps most memorable for shouting, "How dare you! Who the hell do you think you are!" with gritted teeth and fists pumps, targeting the men of his congregation during a Sunday morning sermon at Mars Hill.[22]

---

[21] "After Judge Dismisses Sovereign Grace Lawsuit, Justin Taylor, Kevin DeYoung, and Don Carson Explain Their Silence," *Christianity Today* online, last modified July 22, 2013, https://www.christianitytoday.com/news/2013/may/after-judge-dismisses-sovereign-grace-lawsuit-justin.html.

[22] "Mark Driscoll Screaming How Dare You," YouTube video, 5:50, posted by "JeremyMarriedGuy," April 8, 2009, https://www.youtube.com/watch?v=ZkaeAkJO0w8.

In August of 2014, twenty-one former Mars Hill Church pastors brought forward a plethora of charges against Driscoll, including plagiarism, inappropriate use of church funds, bullying, and his abrasive management style. Dave Kraft, one of the most respected elders involved in the case, brought his own charges a year earlier, citing violations of 1 Timothy 3, Titus 1, and 1 Peter 5.[23] The *New York Times* reported on the story:

> Mr. Driscoll's empire appears to be imploding. He has been accused of creating a culture of fear at the church, of plagiarizing, of inappropriately using church funds and of consolidating power to such a degree that it has become difficult for anyone to challenge or even question him. A flood of former Mars Hill staff members and congregants have come forward, primarily on the Internet but also at a protest in front of the church, to share stories of what they describe as bullying or "spiritual abuse," and 21 former pastors have filed a formal complaint in which they call for Mr. Driscoll's removal as the church's leader.[24]

---

[23] David Kraft, "Statement of Formal Charges and Issues by Pastor Dave Kraft," Patheos, May 10, 2013, http://wp.patheos.com.s3.amazonaws.com/blogs/warrenthrockmorton/files/2014/03/Statement-of-Formal-Charges-and-Issues-by-Pastor-Dave-Kraft.pdf.

[24] Michael Paulson, "A Brash Style That Filled Pews, Until Followers Had Their Fill: Mark Driscoll Is Being Urged to Leave Mars Hill Church," *The New York Times*, August 22, 2014, https://www.nytimes.com/2014/08/23/us/mark-driscoll-is-being-urged-to-leave-mars-hill-church.html.

Shortly afterward on October 14, 2014, Driscoll resigned as pastor in the midst of tremendous angst and frustration by fellow elders and members of his church who had made multiple attempts to call Driscoll to account.[25] Just like C. J. Mahaney, Mark Driscoll eventually left the region and became senior pastor at another church—the Trinity Church in Scottsdale, Arizona.

Even more recently, as noted in the December 29, 2018 issue of World Magazine, James MacDonald, the prominent and well-known pastor of Chicago's Harvest Bible Chapel, was charged by eight former elders of "self-promotion … love of money … domineering and bullying … abusive speech … outbursts of anger … [and] making misleading statements …"[26]

Several weeks later the Chicago Tribune ran a news breaking story with the headline: Harvest Bible Chapel pastor James MacDonald fired: 'A hard but necessary day for our church.'[27]

Unfortunately, until God's people realize that Christ has authorized the collective members of any given church the responsibility and authority to protect itself from such foolishness and harm, men like Mark Driscoll, C. J. Mahaney, James MacDonald, and others will continue to wreak havoc throughout the body of Christ, convinced that they are doing the will of God. Consider this sermon excerpt from Driscoll:

---

[25] For more information on Mark Driscoll and the history of Mars Hill Church, please visit http://marshillrefuge.blogspot.com/p/more-stories.html.
[26] . https://world.wng.org/2018/12/hard_times_at_harvest
[27] Patrick M. O'Connell and Morgan Greene, "Harvest Bible Chapel pastor James MacDonald fired," Chicago Tribune, February 14, 2019, https://www.chicagotribune.com/news/ct-met-harvest-bible-chapel-james-macdonald-turmoil-20190211-story.html.

> Here's what I've learned. You cast vision for your mission, and if people don't sign up, you move on. You move on. There are people that are gonna die in the wilderness, and there are people that are gonna take the hill. That's just how it is. Too many guys waste too much time trying to move stiff necked, stubborn, obstinate people. I am all about blessed subtraction. There is a pile of dead bodies behind the Mars Hill bus [chuckle], and by God's grace, it'll be a mountain by the time we're done. You either get on the bus, or you get run over by the bus. Those are the options. But the bus ain't gonna stop.[28]

Clearly, the residual effects of the Shepherding Movement are still evident in many evangelical churches today, the hallmark of which is a top-down, authoritarian form of church government in which a "lead pastor" rules over the rest of the flock while the members have no real voice or authority to make important decisions in the church (like selecting, challenging, and dismissing leaders—not to mention matters of money and church discipline). In many cases, the members of the church do not recognize the problems with this type of authority structure or polity because they are only taught doctrines *conducive* to a totalitarian and controlling form of government. This conveniently ensures

---

[28] "Mark Driscoll—There is a pile of dead bodies behind the Mars Hill bus," YouTube video, 2:30, posted by "310Revelation," November 3, 2012, https://www.youtube.com/watch?v=BfTmgPhmlto.

the pastor will always have the final word regarding major decisions in the church. Moreover, in today's church climate, the politically correct language of "new and improved" church by-laws and constitutions has sanitized the more toxic and destructive elements of the Shepherding Movement, making it harder to recognize those elements as unorthodox, aberrant, and harmful.

A simple litmus test to determine whether or not a congregation maintains any authority or responsibility regarding its most important decisions (leadership, finances, and church discipline) is to simply ask those in leadership, "Does the congregation/church have authority?" Typically, upon being asked this question, leaders who advocate a top-down, authoritarian form of church government will say something like, "Well, we always desire and seek out the input of our people. We want to know what they think, and we don't make any decisions without their input."

Although this response may initially appease one's questions or concerns, it's not a straightforward answer. If one presses further, one will discover that while many leaders might welcome and eagerly seek input from the congregation, the *leaders* make the decisions in the final analysis. "Opinions," "feedback," and "input" carry no real, effectual, authoritative weight in the decision-making process.

Leaders of such churches will typically smile and nod while they affirm the value and necessity of the church's opinions and input, even though they know it is *they*, the leaders, who will ultimately make the decisions for the church. The congregation is led to believe that this arrangement is completely biblical—they likely have been taught from Hebrews

13:17 that they are duty bound to obey and submit to their leaders without question. We will explore this passage in detail later in the book. Unfortunately, many leaders do not teach on the authority of the church, so congregants are well advised to be more like the Bereans of Acts 17:11, who *searched the Scriptures* rather than accept whatever their leaders said without question.

When leaders fail to teach and affirm the authority of the church, and congregants neglect their responsibility to study church authority (and other relevant topics) for themselves, a host of problems are sure to arise. For example, when my friend Mark, whose story was told in the previous chapter, was privately and publicly disgraced due to the senior pastor's unilateral decision to fire him, a majority of the congregation believed the senior pastor had erred in that decision. However, they also believed they were powerless and impotent to do anything about it. As a result, Mark remained ostracized by the church, suffering severe emotional and spiritual trauma, which eventually led to psychiatric hospitalization. He received no comfort or support from those he had diligently cared for in previous decades because the senior pastor had made it clear to the congregation that this brother had "committed the sin of wicked unbelief."

The letter below is one of many I wrote over the course of several years appealing to other leaders and fellow church members to reconsider the decision made by the senior pastor and to implore members of the congregation to mitigate the harm and abuse done to this beloved brother and his family.

Repentance on the congregation's part was in order, and the restoration of this brother was sorely needed.

Brothers and sisters,

There is a reason why this atrocity has occurred. It occurred because we as a church allowed ourselves to be deceived. I believe this deception has its roots in the Shepherding Movement of the '70s. The fundamental component that marked the Shepherding Movement was the notion that members in the church had no responsibility or authority in managing its own affairs. This was believed to be solely the responsibility and authority of church leaders. Unfortunately, this false teaching/doctrine manifested itself primarily in the practice of "lording over the faith" of the people and resulted in many forms of spiritual abuse against them. I believe this same aberrant church structure and form of polity in turn had a significant influence on the founding leaders of SGM. I believe they subsequently taught and trained their leaders accordingly.

While the current leadership of SGM makes claims they have disassociated themselves from the Shepherding Movement, I believe most of the leaders have failed to desist from many of their harmful practices, specifi-

false and destructive doctrines which have led to this unfortunate situation. Instead, we should take full responsibility for our silence, inaction, and failure to care for our brother and his family, so as to maintain the unity of the faith in the bond of peace. I submit to you, what we have allowed to take place in our congregation is deplorable in the sight of God and grieves the Holy Spirit.

I believe we as the body of Christ have an opportunity to make things right if we allow God to convict our hearts and grace us with the gift of repentance. First, we must ask God for forgiveness for the abdication of our responsibility to love and care for Mark and his family. Second, we must ask Mark and his family for forgiveness for not embracing our responsibility to consider his side of the story, to care for him and his family as Christ would, and make every effort to maintain the unity of the faith and reconciliation.

I submit to you, according to the plain teaching of Scripture, that God has given every local church the authority, autonomy, and responsibility to monitor itself, care for its members, and tend to its own affairs. When a local church ceases to do these things, they cease being a healthy, vibrant, and safe place for its members. The congregation is ultimately its own gatekeeper. No man, council, leader, or convention has been given the sobering responsibility, authority, or calling to impose their will on a congregation. Let us endeavor to honor the Lord in this matter and quickly restore our brother and his family.

Unfortunately, despite this letter of appeal, as well as other pleas for reconciliation from longtime church members, nothing changed. The leaders felt no obligation to address the concerns of the congregation and felt no remorse or compulsion to alter their course of action. This eventually caused a massive church split with deep disillusionment and frustration for the entire congregation. This was profound spiritual abuse—of not just one person but an entire church. Moreover, in the opinion of many other SGM members, it was systemic to the entire SGM organization of churches.

As we have seen in this chapter, the seeds of the Shepherding Movement sown decades before continue to have an adverse effect on many evangelical congregations today, making them impotent and ineffectual to bring about needed reform, especially regarding heavy-handed top-down authoritarian governmental structures in the church. Nevertheless, congregations must embrace their responsibility as the biblical prescription and catalyst for change if reform is to be realized, lest all manner of abuse and harm continue to plague the church.

In light of what is at stake, it is extremely important that we as believers are able to recognize toxic forms of leadership and develop an acute awareness of what constitutes spiritual abuse. To help facilitate this goal, we will turn now to the next chapter.

# Study Notes

# 5

# WHAT IS SPIRITUAL ABUSE?

*Whoever causes one of these little ones who believe in Me to stumble, it would be better for him to have a heavy millstone hung around his neck, and to be drowned in the depth of the sea.*

—Matthew 18:6 (NASB)

*Deception is part of sin's DNA. Sin lies to us. It seeks to convince us that sin brings only pleasure, that it carries no consequences, and that no one will discover it. Sin works hard to make us forget that character, conduct, and consequences are interconnected. And when we neglect this relationship—when we think our sins will not be discovered—we ultimately mock God.*

—C. J. Mahaney, "Hunting Tiger Woods"

The quotation above is from an article C. J. Mahaney wrote in response to Tiger Wood's sex scandal in 2009.[29] I hope the irony

---

[29] "What the adulterer Tiger Woods needs to hear: from C. J. Mahaney," The Domain for Truth (blog), posted by "SLIMJIM," December 10, 2009, https://veritasdomain.wordpress.com/2009/12/10/what-the-adulterer-tiger-woods-need-to-hear-from-c-j-mahaney/.

is not lost on my readers. As noted previously, Mahaney chose to leave the church he had founded instead of staying there to resolve serious concerns voiced by the people he had pastored for almost thirty years. In other words, he *ignored* his own warning regarding the deception of sin. After finding refuge nearby at Capitol Hill Baptist Church, Mahaney eventually relocated several hundred miles away to Louisville, Kentucky, where he began a new church.

In sermons, Mahaney would often tell his former congregation at Covenant Life Church that there was no place else he would rather be. At his departure, many members were left dumbfounded, stunned with disbelief, and flabbergasted by his *lack* of humility, his brazen refusal to humble himself, and the apparent absence of any desire to reconcile with the church he founded so many years before. They and others in the evangelical community could not reconcile Mahaney's behavior with what he had preached and taught for so long—especially his passionate words on humility, transparency, and reconciliation.

Despite this hypocrisy, many prominent evangelical leaders continue to publicly support Mahaney and present him as the personification of a humble leader, even though he showed himself to be like the Scribes and Pharisees of Matthew 23:1–3, where Jesus warns, "Do and observe whatever [the Scribes and Pharisees] tell you, but not the works they do. *For they preach, but do not practice* [emphasis mine]." Likewise, to the consternation and dismay of many, C. J. Mahaney refused to practice what he preached. To add insult to injury, the president of Southern Baptist Theological Seminary, Albert Mohler, along with two other prominent leaders, Mark Dever and Ligon Duncan, all signed a letter drafted by Mohler which defended Mahaney against the allegations of sexual-abuse cover-ups in his SGM network of churches. Here is an excerpt:

> We have stood beside our friend, C. J. Mahaney, and we can speak to his personal integrity. We can make no judgment as to the truthfulness of the horrifying charges of sexual abuse made against some individuals who have been connected, in some way, to Sovereign Grace Ministries and its churches. Our hearts must go out to anyone, and especially to any child, who suffers abuse at the hand of anyone. In such a case the legal authorities must use the full power of the law to investigate and to prosecute any perpetrator of such crimes. *We must take any responsible action to protect the vulnerable, and we must act immediately to inform legal authorities of any charge or claim of sexual abuse, and do so without delay. Our first response must be to call the police, to act to protect the child or young person, and then to proceed to biblical church discipline when the facts demand such a response* [emphasis mine].[30]

By not encouraging Mahaney to return to his church and resolve the serious allegations against him, the authors of this letter, along with other prominent evangelical leaders, enabled

---

[30] Mark Dever, Ligon Duncan, Al Mohler, "Statement," Together for the Gospel, May 23, 2013, https://web.archive.org/web/20130606205256/http://t4g.org/statement/.

Mahaney's irresponsible behavior and thereby became complicit in the pain and devastation suffered by the members of Mahaney's church. All of these men knew better, yet failed to follow their own advice to do what was honorable and right.

Ironically, during the 2011 sex abuse scandal at Pennsylvania State University, Albert Mohler wrote with passion and conviction that he would make absolutely certain that victims of abuse would always be the highest priority and that people with knowledge of abuse should "contact law enforcement authorities without delay." He stated that this would immediately go into effect as the new policy of Southern Baptist Theological Seminary:

> The leaders of Penn State University must have acted, or failed to have acted, out of many motivations. One may well have been to protect the image and reputation of the university. Well, we now see where that leads. A scandal reported and ended in 2002 would be horrible enough. A scandal that began there, was known by officials, and explodes almost a decade later is too horrible to contemplate.
>
> We all need an immediate reality check. I discovered yesterday that the policy handbook of the institution I am proud to lead calls for any employee receiving a report of child abuse, including child sexual abuse, to contact his or her supervisor with that report. That changes today. *The new policy statement will direct employees receiving such a report*

> *to contact law enforcement authorities without delay* [emphasis mine]. Then, after acting in the interests of the child, they should contact their supervisor.
>
> In a real sense, the whole world changed today. We all know more than we knew before, and we are all responsible for that knowledge. The costs of acting wrongly in such a situation, or acting inadequately, are written across today's headlines and the moral conscience of the nation. The tragedy at Penn State is teaching the entire nation a lesson it dare not fail to learn.[31]

Unfortunately, when reports of abuse surfaced against his friend, C. J. Mahaney, Mohler's concern to "contact law enforcement without delay" apparently disappeared. Instead of contacting authorities, Mohler drafted the letter noted previously, publicly *supporting* Mahaney in 2013. This appears to be a double standard and gross hypocrisy.

In late 2018, Mohler raised his standard of accountability even higher when he became aware of sexual abuse allegations within his own denomination, the Southern Baptist Convention (SBC). He passionately insisted that the SBC submit to "an independent, third-party investigation" to properly address the allegations and complaints of sexual abuse within their churches:

---

[31] Albert Mohler, "The Tragic Lessons of Penn State—A Call to Action" (personal website), November 10, 2001, https://albertmohler.com/2011/11/10/the-tragic-lessons-of-penn-state-a-call-to-action/.

cally the insistence of maintaining sole responsibility and authority over the church, which has unfortunately led, in many cases, to (1) lording over the faith of members in the church and (2) various forms of spiritual abuse.

I believe some SGM leaders are convinced it is their responsibility to determine what the will of God is for individual members and then insist those members submit to that will. This is why the leaders of our church did not feel what they had done in pressuring, manipulating, and coercing Mark and his family, as well as other members of the church, was wrong. They were convinced it was their biblical responsibility and had God's authority to do so.

In turn, this deception was taught and propagated throughout our church. The members embraced this false teaching, and we, as a body of believers, became deceived. We believed it was our job as the church to remain passive and silent, even when abuses of power and authority were taking place before our very eyes. On the whole, because we embraced this teaching, we in turn abdicated our God-given responsibility and authority to police and monitor ourselves while ensuring that the unity of the faith in the bond of peace was maintained throughout our membership.

Unfortunately, we believed it was none of the church's business how people were handled by leaders. That was the leadership's job, we erroneously thought. Our job was to submit to what the leadership determined and not challenge or question any of their decisions or actions.

The net result in Mark's case was we as a church, either because of our silence when we knew something was wrong or because we were intentionally kept in the dark for nearly ten years, allowed many grave atrocities to take place that should have never happened.

I believe as a congregation our reasons for inaction were understandably due to what we've been taught. We were simply "submitting to leadership." However, these are not legitimate excuses in the face of the great injustice our brother has suffered. Our only consolation is, *we did not know any better because we were not taught any better.*

Sadly, we operated under misguided and false teaching which allowed these atrocities to take place and persist over a long period of time. We did this because we falsely believed the church has no responsibility or authority in governing its affairs. We were deceived. I trust we are deceived no longer.

In light of these events, I believe we as a church must renounce and repudiate these

# THE URIAH SYNDROME

Sexual misconduct is as old as sin, but the avalanche of sexual misconduct that has come to light in recent weeks is almost too much to bear. These grievous revelations of sin have occurred in churches, in denominational ministries, and even in our seminaries.

Judgment has now come to the house of the Southern Baptist Convention. The terrible swift sword of public humiliation has come with a vengeance. There can be no doubt that this story is not over.

Every Christian church and every pastor and every church member must be ready to protect any of God's children threatened by abuse and must hold every abuser fully accountable. The church and any institution or ministry serving the church must be ready to assure safety and support to any woman or child or vulnerable one threatened by abuse.

The church must make every appropriate call to law enforcement and recognize the rightful God-ordained responsibility of civil government to protect, to investigate, and to prosecute.

A church, denomination, or Christian ministry must look outside of itself when confronted with a pattern of mishandling such responsibilities, or merely of being charged with such a pattern. We cannot vindicate ourselves. That is the advice I have given consistently for many years. I now must make this judgment a matter of public commitment. I believe that any public accusation concerning such a pattern requires an independent, third-party investigation. In making this judgment, I make public what I want to be held to do should, God forbid, such a responsibility arise.[32]

In light of such passionate rhetoric, many hoped that Mohler would acknowledge the glaring discrepancy and hypocrisy between his call for accountability in his own denomination and his failure to publicly challenge C. J. Mahaney and Sovereign Grace Churches to submit to an independent investigation, which had already been spearheaded by Rachel Denhollander and supported by Boz Tchividjian of GRACE ministries. Unfortunately, this was yet to happen.

Several months later, the Houston Chronicle reported on the history of abuse within the SBC:

> Since 1998, roughly 380 Southern Baptist church leaders and volunteers have faced allegations of sexual misconduct, the newspapers found. That includes those who were convicted, credibly accused and successfully sued, and those who confessed or resigned.

---

[32] Albert Mohler, "The Wrath of God Poured Out—The Humiliation of the Southern Baptist Convention" (personal website), May 23, 2018, https://albertmohler.com/2018/05/23/wrath-god-poured-humiliation-southern-baptist-convention/.

More of them worked in Texas than in any other state.

They left behind more than 700 victims, many of them shunned by their churches, left to themselves to rebuild their lives. Some were urged to forgive their abusers or to get abortions.

About 220 offenders have been convicted or took plea deals, and dozens of cases are pending. They were pastors. Ministers. Youth pastors. Sunday school teachers. Deacons. Church volunteers.[33]

When this article was published, Mohler, being challenged with overwhelming evidence and pressure from individuals both inside and outside the SBC, finally conceded to a serious lack of judgment, dismissiveness toward victims of abuse, and a misinformed support of C.J. Mahaney. Sadly, it had been six years since Mohler had drafted the public letter in support of him. As reported by Robert Downen of the Houston Chronicle on February 14, 2019:

> Mohler said he should have been more forceful in his denunciation of Mahaney.
>
> "Yes. Yes. Yes. Yes," [Mohler] said. "I should have been very clear about insist-

---

[33] Robert Downen, Lise Olson, John Tedesco, "Abuse of Faith," Houston Chronicle, February 10, 2019, https://www.houstonchronicle.com/news/investigations/article/Southern-Baptist-sexual-abuse-spreads-as-leaders-13588038.php.

ing on an independent, credible third-party investigation."

"I believe in retrospect I erred in being part of a statement supportive of [Mahaney] and rather dismissive of the charges," Mohler said. "And I regret that action, which I think was taken without due regard to the claims made by the victims and survivors at the time, and frankly without an adequate knowledge on my part, for which I'm responsible."

He added, "I should have said nothing until I had heard from those who were victims and who were making the allegations. I should have sought at that time the advice and counsel of agencies and authorities who were even then on the front lines of dealing with these kinds of allegations."[34]

The next day, Mohler published a statement on the Southern Baptist Theological Seminary (SBTS) website acknowledging his regretful actions and apologizing for how he mishandled issues, stating, "I have recently apologized and asked forgiveness for serious errors I made in how I responded to concerns that were raised about Sovereign Grace Churches and CJ Mahaney."[35]

---

[34] Robert Downen, "Leading Southern Baptist apologizes for supporting leader, church at center of sex abuse scandal," Houston Chronicle, February 14, 2019, https://www.houstonchronicle.com/houston/article/Leading-Southern-Baptist-apologizes-for-13618120.php.

[35] Albert Mohler, "Statement from R. Albert Mohler, Jr. on Sovereign Grace Churches," (personal website), February 15, 2019, http://news.sbts.edu/2019/02/15/statement-r-albert-mohler-jr-sovereign-grace-churches/.

While many are encouraged by these recent statements, it remains to be seen if Mohler will rally together other prominent leaders, who had previously joined him in supporting Mahaney, in order to persuade them to *publicly* challenge Mahaney and Sovereign Grace Churches to *be accountable to the body of Christ by submitting to an independent, third-party investigation.*

This tragic and unfortunate scenario is a sober example of the plight that is sure to befall individual Christians and their congregations when leaders hold greater allegiance to peers and colleagues than the people they are called to care for and protect. Likewise, when church members submit to or tolerate leaders who are encumbered by blind loyalty and misinformation or who motivate through fear, pressure, manipulation, intimidation, and coercion, those congregants inevitably become vulnerable to all forms of abuse.

*Spiritual* abuse, in particular, can be a foreboding precursor to other types of abuse because the spiritual component of an individual is integral to the human constitution. If abusers gain access and control in this area, they can do incredible harm to other areas of one's life.

In fact, just as sexual abusers often "groom" their victims in an effort to gain more and more access to them, abusive spiritual leaders can engage in a similar practice by causing individuals to increasingly compromise their conscience and volition. When physical, sexual, and/or emotional abuse occurs within a Christian context—at church or youth group, for example, or in a Christian family—it is often precipitated by someone who took advantage of the victim's understanding of spiritual authority. People who are perceived as having spiritual authority over others have a greater opportunity to succeed in other forms of abuse. This was famously demonstrated by the mass suicides at Jonestown, the Heaven's Gate cult, and the pervasive sexual abuse in the Roman Catholic Church captured in the film *Spotlight* and, more recently, in an archbishop's allegation that decades of sexual abuse was covered up by church officials, including Pope Francis.[36]

Now we are seeing this malevolent behavior demonstrated in the increasing number of cases of sexual and physical abuse scandals plaguing the evangelical church in America.

## Defining Spiritual Abuse

We can define *spiritual abuse* as "the mistreatment of a person who is in need of help, support or greater spiritual empowerment, with the result of weakening, undermining or decreasing that person's spiritual empowerment." It's a subtle trap in which both the abuser and the victim are locked into patterns of unhealthy beliefs and actions.[37]

Abuse of any kind happens when an individual uses his power over someone else to harm that person. For instance, a physical abuser wields physical power over someone and produces physical wounds, and a sexual abuser wields sexual power over someone and produces sexual wounds. Likewise, a spiri-

---

[36] Edward Pentin, "Ex-Nuncio Accuses Pope Francis of Failing to Act on McCarrick's Abuse," *National Catholic Register*, last modified August 26, 2018, http://www.ncregister.com/daily-news/ex-nuncio-accuses-pope-francis-of-failing-to-act-on-mccarricks-abuse.
Dougherty, Michael Brenden. "The Case Against Pope Francis" *The National Review*, October 29, 2018.

[37] David Johnson and Jeff VanVonderen, *The Subtle Power of Spiritual Abuse* (Bloomington, MN: Bethany House, 1991), 16, 20.

tual abuser uses his spiritual authority to "coerce, control, or exploit a follower," and this produces spiritual wounds.[38]

When people in positions of authority with trustworthy titles—*pastor, elder, bishop, priest, counselor, physician, attorney*—inflict abuse on others, the effects are exponentially devastating because a deep trust has been violated. There is a higher standard of care and confidentiality associated with these professions, usually expressed in a formal code of ethics. These professionals are typically afforded society's highest trust and respect, especially those with the role of spiritual caregiver or "shepherd of God's flock." Therefore, people abused by these professionals can experience profound pain, betrayal, and disillusionment.[39]

Sadly, because of the implicit trust afforded these individuals, victims of spiritual abuse often develop faulty perceptions that the actions of their abusers are legitimate, justified, and even authorized by Scripture. This warped perception continues to enable the abuser and perpetuates more abusive behavior. This happens when abused individuals become unwittingly deceived into believing that the abuser has been authorized by God to exercise spiritual authority over them, which in turn enables other types of abuse to occur.

Those who see the abuse from the outside, like family and friends, find it difficult to understand why the person being taken advantage of does not recognize that he is being abused. This phenomenon of being deceived and losing the ability to recognize abuse is often common to all forms of abuse and

---

[38] Ken Blue, *Healing Spiritual Abuse: How to Break Free from Bad Church Experiences* (Downers Grove, IL: InterVarsity, 1993), 12.

[39] Ronald Enroth, *Recovering from Churches That Abuse* (Grand Rapids, MI: Zondervan, 1994), 16.

produces a sense of entrapment and cognitive dissonance in the victims. They instinctively know something is terribly wrong, but they can't articulate what it is. And they feel powerless to stop it.

Victims of spiritual abuse also typically experience disillusionment and confusion regarding how they perceive God, as well as how they think God perceives them. These debilitating feelings are exacerbated by the barrage of copious Bible passages cited by abusive leaders to justify their behavior and keep their members in line. In the words of Sandra Wilson, author of *Hurt People Hurt People*, these "Bible-beaten folks" see Scripture as "an instrument of torture."[40] Therefore, it is not unusual that spiritual abuse victims are very susceptible to embracing a skewed and jaundiced view of God, leaders, church members, family, and friends.

Accordingly, the deep hurt, anger, depression, anxiety, resentment, and emotional pain that victims may experience often results in the victim distancing himself from God and fellow believers. This can lead to a long-standing aversion to attending church or having anything to do with spiritual matters. These strong feelings and emotions are certainly understandable, but they can also be debilitating and unhealthy. Negative thoughts, feelings, and emotions are not normative, and it is important for those affected by spiritual abuse to know that hope and recovery is possible. God desires for us to be free from the debilitating effects of spiritual abuse so that we can once again love Him and others the way He intended.

---

[40] Sandra D. Wilson, *Hurt People Hurt People: Hope and Healing for Yourself and Your Relationships* (Grand Rapids: Discovery House, 2001), 189.

# THE URIAH SYNDROME

To that end, there is hope for those traumatized by spiritual abuse, and there are steps one can take to facilitate healing and recovery. The first and most important step is to remove oneself from the environment and culture where the abuse occurred. Afterward, one should seek professional counseling and begin to process what happened, why it happened, and how to prevent it from happening in the future. As a victim of abuse undergoes the process of healing, he will learn to recognize and discern the common traits and characteristics of abusers.

## Characteristics of Spiritual Abusers

Spiritual abusers are often charismatic, personable, charming, and funny. They tend to have "type A" personalities and often exhibit narcissistic behavior and thought patterns. They typically portray themselves as superior to others and are offended (or find it difficult to believe) when anyone resists or defies their teaching or counsel. They are diplomatic and friendly in public but, behind closed doors, can be vicious and vindictive. If their teaching or behavior is ever challenged—which is rare, since abusers are masters at intimidation—they will redefine terms, deny accusations, and/or insist that their accusers are divisive and rebellious. Spiritually abusive people are adept at "turning the tables" and making their accusers feel like they are the problem and should be subject to church discipline if their accusations continue. One will likely feel confused, befuddled, and hoodwinked after confronting a spiritually abusive individual.

Another characteristic common to spiritual abusers is their propensity to project an attractive image of superior skills, abilities, and accomplishments. These skills could be either natural or supernatural in nature. The image created by these supposed superior abilities may appear genuine and impressive at first, but further discernment often reveals an underlying tendency to manipulate and deceive others. How often have we heard of someone with an amazing prophetic or healing gift, only to eventually find out he used his gifts to manipulate and control others? What about prosperity preachers who claim the promise of special blessings and healing in exchange for monetary donations? Or leaders who boast of possessing a special anointing, spiritual power, or dynamic speaking ability that elevates them above fellow believers? The spiritual abuse these leaders propagate can likewise be difficult to detect as it is often couched in simple, unassuming language and marked by veiled efforts at diplomacy with subtle forms of emotional manipulation.

For example, the pastor of my former church made a concerted effort to dismiss his intimidating and manipulative teaching style by calling it "unintentional legalism" and refused to acknowledge that what he had actually engaged in was lording over others, which is spiritual abuse. To admit one is guilty of "legalism" might sound noble and contrite, but the term is too vague to refer to specific behavior since it is a noun and does not denote a specific action. On the other hand, *lording over* is a verb phrase that *does* refer to specific behavior; namely, persuading, coercing, or manipulating congregants to follow or embrace a leader's agenda or gain God's acceptance based on works. This behavior by leaders usually results in members of the congregation being motivated by fear, not faith, and fosters a performance-based culture of legalism that leads to profound spiritual abuse if left unaddressed. Legalism, then, is the *fruit* or *result* of lording over others.

I wrote my pastor a letter challenging him to distinguish between these two terms and asked him to forward the letter to the rest of our leadership team. To my knowledge, the letter was never forwarded. Neither did I receive any response other than a veiled accusation that I was being divisive and rebellious. This response produced fear and pressure to conform to his assessment, and it illustrates why it is important to pay attention to any reservations the Holy Spirit might manifest in your heart and mind when interacting with a spiritually abusive leader. You should be particularly wary if you come away from a teaching or message feeling pressured, intimidated, or manipulated. Don't discount those feelings. You might not be able to articulate the unrest in your heart, but you'll have a profound sense that something is very wrong.

Abusive leaders can also dismiss normative biblical principles in order to accommodate their own agendas. This can be seen in the following exchange I had with the senior pastor who had dismissed my friend Mark. The senior pastor had been hard-pressed for over a year by three laypeople to come clean about Mark's public shaming and dismissal. I was a church deacon at this time. In this first letter, the senior pastor tried to persuade the deacons to yield our concerns to an outside third-party mediator rather than to follow the precepts of Matthew 18, which would mean resolving the issue through the church itself. By taking this route, the pastor was seeking to maintain control and minimize exposure of his wrongdoing by keeping everyone else in the church in the dark. My comments on his letter below are in brackets.

Gentlemen,

I'm writing to appeal that you join us in mediation with an impartial mediator. I ask because I value our relationships and genuinely believe a mediator could help us navigate through the issues that are currently separating us. Based on our recent interactions, I don't believe that is possible at present without outside help [translation: outside the help of the *congregation*]. The areas where we have disagreements on facts and interpretations continues to grow and, like times in a marriage, we've reached a point where we are in need of a mediator's objective wisdom to hear one another [implying that the congregation does not possess any "objective wisdom to hear one another"].

The relational commitments we all agreed upon four years ago [signed legal documents ensuring that members would not sue the church] were adopted to provide clarity and direction for challenging circumstances like the ones we face today. It seemed wise to make provision ahead of time so that if a mediator ever became necessary, a process would already be in place. These are issues that can be sorted out by a *professional mediator* [but not the congregation] in an expeditious way, and our desire would be to walk through this process quickly and redemptively. But the benefit largely lies in your willingness to partner with us in the process of mediator selection and intervention. Please consider this and let me know your thoughts ASAP.

The mediator had already been contacted and given possible meeting dates. Ultimately, these individuals/deacons had absolutely no bearing on whether or not an outside mediator would be utilized. The pastor just needed them to feel like they were instrumental in his decision. Here was my response:

Pastor,

I do not believe the issues are confusing, ambiguous, or lacking in clarity. They only appear to be so when Mark and I are not present to substantiate or deny what is being said. I believe Mark has requested a very reasonable and biblical solution [which was to allow the deacons to hear the complaint]. I trust my brothers [the deacons] implicitly to remain "impartial" and arrive at a God-glorifying solution once we have had a full hearing [which was to allow a larger segment of the church to hear the alleged charges].

Actually, I believe that asking a third-party mediator into our church's family business is an insult to the spiritual aptitude of the church, and now to these men. I continue to be bombarded by e-mails and calls from church members asking for an "open and transparent" forum to participate in.

As I understand it, you have stated that Mark has "ought" against you and that this is why we need a mediator. I take strong issue with this. Think about what you are saying. Since when do we call a mediator into our church family over something as fundamentally relational as this? The church cannot take much more vacillating or procrastination. We need to simply do what the Scriptures call for, which has never been done: to "tell it to the church" (Matthew 18:17).

Mark's idea is in keeping with the spirit of Matthew 18, which the pastors know we are attempting to abide by, and have been making this effort for more than a year now. The church is not even aware of this. Nor are they aware of the charges that were brought forward. The deacons seem to be willing to exercise their responsibility in the fear of God.

Once again, I have full confidence that, collectively, these men have the necessary stature and spiritual caliber to help us navigate through this issue. We do not need "professional mediators" to sort out our problems. God has great confidence the local church is well equipped to settle such matters.

activity or skill mastered, we earned a metal pin—I learned that a pure young woman should save even kissing until marriage, should be homeschooled and homespun, and should dream of being a stay-at-home mother of many children. Godly girls should aspire to be meek, submissive, nurturing, and to pray for our future husbands, who would lead and protects us.

When I think of the little girl with a paisley bonnet hung around her neck and a jean dress catching between her calves who thought that "modest was hottest," I wonder what these men were supposed to lead us to or protect us from. Perhaps themselves. Over the years, I've learned to turn a blind eye on the sheep. They walk themselves off cliffs.

Children who experience cynicism and depression as a result of exposure to spiritual abuse feel the personal violation of being controlled, manipulated, or "lorded over" by someone they perceive as a spiritual leader who represents God. As a result, they then often form a perverted and skewed perspective of God, assigning Him inaccurate character qualities. They have a tendency to believe that God is a hard taskmaster who is never satisfied and whose love, affection, and acceptance is conditional and based on their performance. When spiritually abusive leaders perpetuate a legalistic and performance-based culture from the pulpit, it can produce a trickle-down effect in which parents themselves begin to cultivate a performance-based love relationship with their children at home. In my opinion, the most important and immediate intervention strategy that parents can implement for their children is to remove them from spiritually abusive environments and begin cultivating a parent-child relationship based on unconditional love.

In addition to producing depression and cynicism, spiritual abuse has contributed to divorce, strained family relationships, and the loss of long-standing friendships. Some victims have even taken (or sought to take) their own lives in an effort to find the ultimate reprieve from their pain and depression, as this excerpt from an anonymous letter reveals:

> We knew when SGM was lying to us but trusted that they were our God-ordained leaders. [They] made sure that there was an endless procession of "praise" reports and testimonies to quell our concerns.
>
> It was a strange thing to first experience freedom from SGM in the limited fashion of knowing that I could take my own life. It was the first time in many years that I felt, well, human again. I had a choice, and therefore no longer felt trapped by these SGM men.
>
> The best thing was that it was Christ and Christ alone that took me from that darkness—no church, no pastors, no brothers. There were plenty of brothers around, but their words had no meaning at the time.

Just His word on my nightstand next to the would-be object of my mortal death.[41]

The letter above was addressed to an organization called Ambassadors of Reconciliation (AoR), which, ironically, was founded "to help Christians and their churches in carrying out their peacemaking responsibilities as Christ's ambassadors [and] equipping Christians and their churches for living, proclaiming and cultivating lifestyles of reconciliation."[42] AoR was hired by SGM, the network of churches to whom I previously belonged, ostensibly to help SGM members reconcile numerous grievances and complaints pertaining to SGM leadership. Hiring outside third-party mediators is a common practice among spiritually abusive leaders and organizations. They seldom spare no expense to hire third-party entities as mediators but will refuse to dialogue or be transparent with the congregation itself. This prevents the church from fulfilling its biblical responsibility to adjudicate its own affairs privately and is a convenient method whereby leadership can avoid the public scrutiny of the congregation. As a result, these third-party mediators often do more harm than good. Many SGM members who participated in interviews with AoR felt this was the case.

Many SGM leaders had previously demonstrated a long history of lording over their congregants as evidenced by the large numbers of people who either wrote letters to AoR or showed up in person at SGM's founding church to commu-

---

[41] "Let's Help Ted Kober," SGM Survivors, comment posted by "Unassimilated," October 8, 2001, 3:15 p.m., http://www.sgmsurvivors.com/2011/10/15/lets-help-ted-kober/.

[42] "About Us," Ambassadors of Reconciliation, accessed June 25, 2018, https://www.hisaor.org/web-content/AboutUs.html.

nicate their complaints. They hoped AoR would address the bullish and abusive behavior demonstrated by SGM leaders. Unfortunately, in the opinion of many congregants who met with AoR representatives, AoR failed miserably to adequately address what these members perceived to be systemic abuse that permeated the SGM culture.

Moreover, after pouring their hearts out to AoR "counselors" in hopes of finding some reprieve for the many wrongs they had suffered, AoR compounded their frustration and discouragement by showing a complete lack of sensitivity toward those who courageously decided to attend the sessions.

For example, when AoR had agreed on a meeting place and time in order to listen to those who wanted to voice their grievances, the venue chosen happened to be the very church where much of the alleged abuse had taken place! More astonishingly, the time and place was scheduled at the same location where all the pastors in SGM would be simultaneously meeting for an SGM pastors' conference! Therefore, there was a very high probability that those who came to voice their concerns would likely be seen by the very pastors who had perpetrated their abuse! In fact, the night of our interview, I remember seeing my own former pastor and his wife in the waiting area as I peered through the small glass window in the door as we were concluding our interview, and had to ask the AoR counselor to escort them down the hall so my wife and I could leave in private.

Yet, I had written AoR weeks before communicating my concern that this type of situation should be avoided. Since I was a mental health counselor who had worked with many of the attendees, I was concerned about the intimidation, stress, and breach of confidentiality this venue would impose on those who decided to step forward and tell their stories. So I wrote to AoR and asked them to consider moving the venue to a different location. Unfortunately, I never received a response, and the interviews were performed as planned.

In my opinion, many people chose not to meet with AoR that day specifically because of the venue. Shortly after the AoR meetings took place, a plethora of comments were posted at SGM Survivors that reflected the indignation and profound disappointment by those who bravely chose to attend the interviews.[43]

As word got out about the pervasive spiritual abuse propagated by SGM against its own pastors and members, other leaders began to weigh in, appalled by these revelations. Upon my submitting an academic paper[44] that chronicled the atrocious spiritual abuse of one of my own former pastors, a professor at Liberty University responded:

> Highlighting the significance of spiritual concerns by the American Counseling Association Code of Ethics, the American Association of Christian Counselors Code of Ethics, and the Diagnostic and Statistical Manual caught my attention regarding the paper's topic. Without any subtypes to fit this issue of spiritual abuse, it does seem appro-

---
[43] For more information, please visit www.sgmsurvivors.com and search for "Ambassadors of Reconciliation."
[44] "Spiritual Abuse as a Component of Post-Traumatic Stress Syndrome," available as an appendix in this book.

priate to place it with post-traumatic stress disorder.

As a pastor myself, the story of John brought tears to my eyes. It really seemed as if the program was valued more than the person, leading to a brutal experience. The impact of the trauma was also very apparent in how it affected his family. The pain overflowed to others close to him, multiplying the trauma. To be honest, I felt I could sense your own passion over this issue throughout the paper.

Creating clarity between "lording over" and "legalism" helped me better understand how a leader might pull someone into the unhealthy influence of spiritual abuse. It reminded me of when Jesus said, "Woe to you, teachers of the law and Pharisees, you hypocrites! You travel over land and sea to win a single convert, and when he becomes one, you make him twice as much a son of hell as you are" (Matthew 23:15, NIV). Jesus really brings to light how sinister religious sin and abuse can be. My heart goes out to John. Your paper has inspired me to share the love of Christ rather than the lording of religion. Thank you!

Fortunately, the problem of spiritual abuse is gaining increased recognition in the field of mental health. New and innovative therapeutic techniques, models, diagnostic considerations, and treatment interventions are presently being researched and considered in order to offer relevant and therapeutic remedies to those who suffer from the trauma of spiritual abuse.[45]

In this chapter, I've sought to define spiritual abuse and show the extent to which it harms individuals and congregations throughout the body of Christ. It is typically propagated by errant leaders whose preaching and practice have caused the faith of many Christians to be shipwrecked and destroyed. We have considered several examples that reflect the insidious nature of spiritual abuse and have seen the devastation it can cause if left unchecked. Most importantly, we've recognized that those who insist on practicing abusive leadership in the church are in blatant contradiction to the teaching and ministry of Christ.

But how do such atrocities find their way into the church? What precipitates and allows for such a toxic culture of spiritual abuse to take root in a congregation? How can we prevent it from happening? In the next chapter, we will answer these and other questions, and we'll begin by considering one of the most insidious, subtle culprits of abuse: *deception*.

---

[45] Eliezer Witztum, Review of *Religion and Spirituality in Psychiatry*, edited by Philippe Huguelet and Harold G. Koenig, *Mental Health, Religion & Culture* 14, no. 1 (January 2011): 79–81, https://www.tandfonline.com/doi/abs/10.1080/13674676.2010.535318.

# Study Notes

# 6

# THE CHURCH: ASLEEP AT THE WHEEL

*For the time is coming when people will not endure sound teaching, but having itching ears they will accumulate for themselves teachers to suit their own passions, and will turn away from listening to the truth and wander off into myths.*
—2 Timothy 4:3–4

*There is no doubt about it, recognizing you were deceived, manipulated, and controlled is enraging. What a sense of being lied to and of being conned! What a sense of being deceived! For many, it is a sense of violation akin only to rape—the rape of the mind.*
—Wendy Ford, *Recovery from Abusive Groups*

In 1973, Wendy Ford was recruited into a Bible-based cult where she remained for seven years before finally being set free after two separate deprogramming efforts helped dissuade her from the beliefs she was indoctrinated into. After leaving the cult and going through a lengthy process of recovery, Ford has been able to help many others navigate the difficulties of leaving cultic organizations and begin the road to recovery. For those adversely affected by spiritual abuse, her analogy comparing it to rape is not an overstatement, as evidenced by the increasing mental-health issues associated with such abuse.[46]

The perilous journey of spiritual abuse often begins when we subject ourselves to the subtle influence, manipulation, and teachings of misguided leaders. When we become convinced that the messages we hear from these leaders (and the church culture they help create) are harmless and even endorsed by God as good, true, and healthy, then deception has firmly taken root. At that point, we are embracing something false as true, and it affects our entire worldview, especially our perception of God, the Bible, and the church. Our mischaracterization of God will lead us to believe in a performance-based, legalistic paradigm of spirituality, which we will adamantly defend and propagate with "proof texts" from Scripture so that every area of our lives will be affected by this skewed perspective of God.

Tragically, this often ruptures friendships and family relationships and is usually exacerbated by any efforts to convince the misguided person that he has been deceived. In fact, he will typically believe these actions prove the *legitimacy* of his new beliefs and lifestyle. He sees himself as being persecuted by his family and friends for standing firm in the truth as a valiant warrior who remains loyal to his organization. He genuinely believes it is *others*, like his family and friends, who are deceived. Extricating an individual from this kind of deception

---

[46] Wendy Ford, *Recovery from Abusive Groups: Healing from the Trauma of Authoritarian Leaders* (Bonita Springs, FL: American Family Foundation, 1993), 45–46.

> Our deacons are not inferior in any way to this mediator. In my view, they have been chosen for such a time as this. I hope they step up to the challenge. I know the rest of the church is waiting and hoping these men will do just that.
>
> Please, let's not disappoint or unnecessarily insult and isolate our entire church by opting for a mediator instead of the gifts, callings, and aptitude God has provided in these men and our congregation.

Ultimately, the pastor's recommendations were followed, and the third-party mediation took months to conclude, using over $14,000 of the church's money. Within three months, approximately 75 percent of the congregation left. Soon afterward, the pastor was caught in a public scandal involving personal moral failure. He refused to address this issue in a biblical manner and eventually moved to another town. The church has never recovered.

## The Effects of Spiritual Abuse on Children

Children and adolescents who have been spiritually abused bear a unique burden since children are developmentally in a more vulnerable position than adults and deeply rely on authority figures. One of the most troubling repercussions of spiritual abuse in children and adolescents is *depression*, ranging from mild cases to those requiring psychiatric hospitalization. In my own counseling experience, I have found in nearly every case that this type of depression is rooted in the exposure to a legalistic church and family culture characterized by a performance-based relationship toward God and others. This inevitably results in children becoming more sin-conscious than grace-conscious and produces a pervasive feeling of not being able to "measure up," which casts a perpetual pall over their lives. Often these children are prone to being fearful, people-pleasing, and very susceptible to peer pressure. They are usually confused or cynical regarding the nature and character of God and feel that nothing they do is sufficient in gaining a sense of pleasure and acceptance from Him. Consider these words shared with me by a homeschooled teenage girl who grew up in an abusive church and discovered her former pastor had been caught soliciting a prostitute and who then abandoned the congregation instead of submitting to biblical discipline:

> I felt a chronic anger at men who blamed women for their lust as if they were blind sheep being led astray by the hemline of a dress—at a church and community of people that told girls who had not even reached puberty that they were "stumbling blocks" to men their fathers' ages—that to dress a certain way or to walk or talk too confidently would make them sin.
>
> The pastor's daughter and I learned how to be good housewives. Innocent shrieks at tiny roses twirled out of pink frosting drowned out the light worship music that drifted from a nearby CD player. For every

is a daunting task and involves much prayer, patience, and the merciful intervention of God.

# Deception

A basic definition of what it means to be spiritually deceived is when someone successfully convinces you that a false interpretation or teaching from Scripture is actually true and should therefore be embraced and applied in your life. When we believe something from the Bible to be true when it is actually false, then we are deceived. Often, the individual propagating this false belief genuinely believes that his interpretation or understanding is without error and is biblically sound. Careful study of the Scriptures, however, will determine the veracity of his statements. Just because we (or our leaders) adamantly believe something to be true does not make it so. A teaching from the Bible may often sound true and convincing at first, only to be revealed as false and harmful after closer scrutiny.

Usually, the person who is teaching something false from the Bible has *already* been deceived and sincerely believes what he is telling you is true. His intention is not necessarily to deceive you—his intention is to convince you to believe the "truth." He knows that if you accept what he is saying as true, then he will have authority, control, and power over you. He must convince you that *you* are the one who is deceived and mistaken in your beliefs and therefore should embrace his paradigm of what is actually true. Otherwise, he would lose the means by which to control you and would have to face the prospect of his own deception. This is precisely why many leaders who teach false doctrines related to authority in the church will not admit they are in error but will go down with the ship. They would rather sacrifice an entire congregation than acknowledge their error.

Moreover, it's important to note that when deception occurs, two things must symbiotically exist: (1) a false message and (2) our *choice to believe* in that false message. When we fall prey to deception, we *exercise our own volition* to believe something false is true. Most deception can be avoided by simply doing what the Bible encourages us to do—to test all things and to search the Scriptures to see if what is being said is true or not. Again, we become spiritually deceived when we believe something that contradicts what the Bible teaches. This is why those who want to help free others from abusive groups must be excellent students of the Bible. Ultimately, it is only by knowing the truth that we can enjoy true freedom (John 8:32). We can also be encouraged by the promise that the Holy Spirit is our Teacher, and He will only affirm what is actually true (John 14:26).

For many areas of our Christian experience, our beliefs have profound repercussions on our spiritual health and the health of the congregations to which we belong. To illustrate the importance of this point, I'd like you to participate in a short self-assessment. The statements below are very relevant to issues of spiritual abuse. Consider whether each sentence is true or false. Your responses will likely indicate whether you are prone to deception and therefore susceptible to spiritual abuse. Remember, your answers must be biblically informed and verifiable.

\_\_\_ There is hierarchy in the Church.
\_\_\_ The Bible teaches that my pastor is my primary teacher.

\_\_\_ I should view my pastor as a "spiritual father" or the "head of the church."
\_\_\_ Those in leadership have authority over the congregation.
\_\_\_ If I don't obey the leaders, I am disobeying God.
\_\_\_ Leaders will give an account to God regarding how well I obeyed and submitted to their leadership.
\_\_\_ The Bible says I have to obey and submit to leaders unconditionally.
\_\_\_ It's appropriate for leaders to tell me whom to vote for, whom I should date, whom I should marry, how I should raise my children, where I should work, where I should go to college, who my friends should be, and how I should spend my free time.
\_\_\_ Leaders are more spiritual and are able to hear God better than I can.
\_\_\_ I'm rebellious and divisive if I respectfully disagree with those in leadership.
\_\_\_ It's not all right to "agree to disagree" with a leader.
\_\_\_ There are no disputable matters in the Bible.
\_\_\_ Leaders determine where I fit in the body of Christ
\_\_\_ Leaders determine what small group or ministry I should join.
\_\_\_ It's not my place to speak up if I hear something questionable taught from the pulpit.
\_\_\_ It's not my responsibility to say when I feel someone is being unfairly treated by leaders.
\_\_\_ It's not my responsibility to be involved in choosing leaders.
\_\_\_ It's not my responsibility to know financial details about my church.
\_\_\_ It's not my responsibility to correct a leader.

___ It's not my responsibility to be involved in the weighty decisions of my church.
___ It's not my responsibility to know the details of a leader's removal or termination.
___ Leaders are not subject to church discipline.
___ It's none of my business how much leaders are paid.
___ It's none of my business how my church spends its money.
___ It's none of my business who joins my church.
___ It's none of my business if the leaders ask someone to leave my church.
___ It's acceptable for a leader to publicly disparage or impugn the character of another member.
___ Leaders can share concerns with the congregation about "problematic members," but members shouldn't share concerns about "problematic leaders."
___ Leaders determine when someone is repentant or not.
___ Leaders determine when or if someone should be restored to my church.
___ Leaders determine how much I should give financially above and beyond my tithe.
___ It's the leader's business to know how much I give.
___ I'm sinning if I don't give at least 10 percent of my income to my church.
___ Leaders determine what my church's bylaws and constitution will be.
___ If a leader says I should sign a "covenant agreement," I should do it.
___ Leaders are always right.
___ Leaders have the ultimate authority in my church.
___ The church has no authority.

____ Basically, my job as a member of the church is to show up on Sunday, pay my tithe, and serve whenever and wherever I'm told.

## "Love Bombing"

One of the most common experiences of people who join an abusive or cultic group is an exaggerated affection, care, and hospitality shown to them when they first consider joining the group. This is known as "love bombing" and creates a feeling of total acceptance, along with the promise of future positive, significant friendships. Because these groups encourage and reinforce naive and childlike thinking and will speak of broad ideas like unity, salvation, or world peace with little to no critical evaluation, one's decision to become a member tends to be likewise uninformed and spontaneous.[47]

Though "love bombing" is more often associated with non-Christian groups, the evangelical Christian community seems to have developed its own version of this behavior. In Christian groups, it is very difficult to determine whether or not this behavior is a precursor to abuse since it is very similar to the kind of behavior that members of a healthy church are encouraged to engage in (e.g., loving one another [John 13:34], comforting others [2 Cor. 1:4], being hospitable [Titus 1:8], and laying down our lives for our friends [John 15:12–13]).

How can you tell whether this behavior will turn abusive? It's all about *motivation*. An abusive church's or leader's motiva-

---

[47] Mark I. Sirkin, "Cult involvement: A systems approach to assessment and treatment," *Psychotherapy: Theory, Research, Practice, Training 27*, no. 1 (1990): 116–123, http://psycnet.apa.org/record/1990-17899-001.

tion is primarily to gain loyalty, submission, and control over the congregation. This creates an abnormal and unhealthy dependence on others, particularly leaders, and facilitates the acceptance of and adherence to the group's values and ideology. A healthy church's motivation, on the other hand, is the promotion of spiritual health and freedom in Christ with a view toward spiritual maturity. This ultimately results in a greater dependence on Christ, which facilitates one's willful acceptance and adherence to God and His Word.

For example, let's say other church members urge you to attend a midweek meeting on how to raise children. Why? Is it because the church expects you to incorporate their particular teaching about raising children into your own family? Or do they want you to attend because they simply believe the teaching will help you become better parents? These are two very different motivations.

Unfortunately, "love bombing" from an abusive group commonly causes its committed members to become very defensive, angry, and even hostile toward anyone who questions the group's motivation, authenticity, and sincerity of care and love. When a member decides to leave, he quickly discovers that the people whom he thought had unconditionally loved him now shun and scold him. Even with this revelation, many ex-members find it very difficult to believe negative feedback about the group.[48]

People subjected to this kind of behavior from their supposed friends, family, and brethren in Christ are usually devastated since those whom they once considered close companions now treat them as treacherous and disloyal. I've counseled

---

[48] Ibid.

many of these survivors, and they tell me they felt like their heart was being ripped out. They felt abandoned by the people closest to them. Many of them manifest features and traits of post-traumatic stress disorder (PTSD). When I think of their sorrow, I'm reminded of David's lament in Psalm 55:

> For it is not an enemy who taunts me—
> then I could bear it;
> it is not an adversary who deals insolently with me—
> then I could hide from him.
> But it is you, a man, my equal,
> my companion, my familiar friend.
> We used to take sweet counsel together;
> within God's house we walked in the throng.[49]

Another common practice found in abusive groups is the tendency to view a male leader as a father figure or "head" of the church. Such a leader may tell his congregation, "We're a big family, and I'm going to speak to you as a father would to his children." This kind of statement seems innocent, but the Bible says, "Call no man your father on earth, for you have one Father, who is in heaven" (Matt. 23:8–9). When I myself once heard a pastor speak of his church as a family, I asked him what role he perceived himself to play in that family. He answered immediately—the father. It was evident from his speech, tone of voice, demeanor, and previous behavior that he ascribed a higher authority to himself as the "father" of that church. I believe this was also an example of *grooming*, discussed in the previous chapter, in which a leader begins to foster a percep-

---
[49] Psalm 55:12–4.

tion among his congregation that he is superior in position, title, and authority—all with the intent of taking advantage of this perception for his own benefit. That is the problem with a leader who presents himself as a father to the congregation: he promotes an elevated authority and hierarchy which the Bible warns against. Rather, Scripture consistently treats all church members as having equal value and authority since God shows no partiality (Acts 10:34) and does not allow hierarchies to exist in church government (Matt. 20:25–26).

## Do You Have a High View of the Church?

While it's important to cultivate a genuine knowledge of biblical truth, as well as maintain a biblical perception of our leaders, it is equally important to have a biblical perception of the church as a whole. Do you truly believe it is the body of Christ on the earth today—the "fullness of Him who fills all in all" (Eph. 1:23)? Did you know that Jesus so closely identifies Himself with the church that He calls it by His own name? In Acts 9:3–6, while Saul was continuing to persecute the church, Jesus suddenly appeared and asked, "Why are you persecuting Me?" Now, Jesus had already ascended into heaven by this time and was no longer walking on earth. How then could Saul have been persecuting Him? After all, Saul was persecuting *Christians*. But when Saul asked who it was that he was persecuting, Jesus responded, "I am Jesus, whom you are persecuting." This truth and its repercussions are amazing to consider—we are, corporately, the *body of Christ* on the earth!

Along with His name, Jesus has given the church everything needed for life and godliness,[50] an ability to make righteous and wise judgments,[51] and gifts that enable us to care for one another and reach the lost.[52] He assures us that we can hear His voice as we pray[53] and that one day we shall see Him face-to-face.[54] Indeed, Jesus has great confidence in the church and has equipped her for every good work.[55] Through both peril and peacetime, He promises He will build her up and uphold her by His mighty right hand[56] so that even the gates of hell would not stop her advance.[57] Jesus has lavishly equipped and empowered His church, and He has the utmost confidence that His body, manifested in a local congregation, is able to hear His voice, discern His will, and make weighty decisions that require the wisdom and counsel of God. The church is the pillar and foundation of the truth,[58] a stalwart bulwark in perilous times and a noble bride meant to reflect the beauty and holiness of the Bridegroom.[59] Jesus has given the church his name, His message, and His mission. He has given her His gifts along with the power of His mighty Spirit to accomplish all that He calls her to do. He has commissioned her to be a light in darkness, a city set on a hill,[60] and a testimony of Himself to a dying and

---

[50] 2 Peter 1:3
[51] 1 Corinthians 5:12
[52] Romans 12:6–8
[53] John 10:27–28
[54] Revelation 22:4
[55] 2 Timothy 3:16–17
[56] Isaiah 41:10
[57] Matthew 16:18
[58] 1 Timothy 3:15
[59] Ephesians 5:25, Revelation 19:7–8
[60] Matthew 5:14

desperate world. After all, the same power that raised Christ from the dead dwells in His people![61]

Clearly, Jesus has tremendous confidence in the church—but do we? When I talk with Christians who have been disillusioned and disappointed by their church experiences, I often hear these complaints about their church leaders:

> *They* were too overbearing.
> *They* made all the ministry decisions.
> *They* fired longtime elders without asking anyone's opinion or counsel.
> *They* excommunicated people without our knowledge.
> *They* insinuated that we were deserting the church if we moved out of town.
> *They* expected us to be transparent about *our* sins and failures, but *they* were never open or honest about *their* own shortcomings.
> *They* didn't talk much about the love of God, but they sure talked a lot about our sinfulness and how we needed to constantly improve.

In counseling, we call these types of remarks *blame-shifting*. That's when someone who should take responsibility for his own thoughts and behavior blames another person instead. Too many people in the body of Christ have unwittingly adopted this mind-set when it comes to matters of church authority and responsibility. They abdicate their duty to be the final authority on church matters and choose to acquiesce to intimidating and manipulative leaders—then they blame those leaders for abu-

---

[61] Romans 8:11

sive behavior! Many churches have thus become impotent and anemic to bring about necessary change and reform.

This happens when congregations are systematically and thoroughly convinced that their leaders are the only ones with the authority and power to conduct the affairs of the church. When this occurs, the congregation is unfortunately "asleep at the wheel," allowing unnecessary harm to befall the flock. Sadly, the church in these cases has succumbed to the same demeaning perspective of the Israelites in Numbers 13:33, who fearfully saw themselves as weak grasshoppers in the face of their enemy. If this perception rings true regarding your own church experience, you are likely being led by leaders who teach and propagate a low view of the church but a very high view of leadership, and I submit that the reason for this disparity is that *it allows leaders to maintain power and control over a congregation* through a subtle indoctrination of subjugation.

Any leader who promotes the idea that the church (or a local congregation) should submit itself to the authority of a few select individuals is fostering a concept contrary to Scripture because he is failing to submit himself to the proper biblical authority: *the congregation*, who is the body of Christ. Moreover, since Christ's authority is manifested in the church, these leaders are actually *usurping the authority of Christ*. They are placing themselves above the body of Christ in a place of headship exclusively reserved for Christ Himself (Col. 1:18). This is a very serious problem for these leaders, as well as the congregations who allow it to happen.

Too often, the glorious, high view of the church held by Christ and the Scriptures gets turned on its head, and the body of Christ is duped into believing that laypeople in the congregation are under a biblical obligation to adhere to a top-down form of church government, which leaves everyone marginalized except for the leaders. This is taught *nowhere* in Scripture and clearly contradicts Jesus when He specifically addresses church authority and how leaders are to function:

> You know that the rulers of the Gentiles lord it over them, and their great ones exercise authority over them. *It shall not be so among you.* But whoever would be great among you must be your servant. (Matt. 20:25–26, emphasis mine)

This teaching was important enough to appear in three out of the four Gospels.[62] Here, Christ calls attention to the typical authority structure of His day, then unequivocally states that His church will not practice this same type of authority structure. Church leadership is not about exercising authority or control over others by virtue of one's role, function, position, title, or gifting.

True leadership in the church is about being a *servant*.

This is exactly why Christ Himself intentionally took the lowest position of a foot washer to make certain His disciples and future leaders in the church clearly understood His expectation for how leadership should function in His church (John 13:12–17). Moreover, you will find through careful study that Scripture consistently shows a sober respect and high view of the church in which leaders do not "lord over" others but work *with* them for love's sake (2 Cor. 1:24).

---

[62] Matthew 20:25–26, Mark 10:42–43, and Luke 22:25–26

I hope this chapter has helped develop a renewed appreciation for the stature and responsibility of the local church, along with a sobering realization of the authority and power a local church must exercise to ensure the well-being of its members. Perhaps you find yourself with such an opportunity to participate in making fundamental changes and reforms in your own church that will significantly impact its life and health. To that end, I've included a letter of my own at the back of this book that you may use as a template to help communicate these ideas.

In the coming chapters, we will consider the biblical warrant for the congregation's responsibility and authority to manage and arbitrate its own affairs. This will point to *polity*—how a church governs itself. However, as we will see in the next chapter, polity is not the fundamental problem; neither is it necessarily the solution.

# Study Notes

# 7

# POLITY IS NOT THE PROBLEM

*If your brother sins against you, go and tell him his fault, between you and him alone. If he listens to you, you have gained your brother. But if he does not listen, take one or two others along with you, that every charge may be established by the evidence of two or three witnesses. If he refuses to listen to them, tell it to the church. And if he refuses to listen even to the church, let him be to you as a Gentile and a tax collector.*
—Matthew 18:15–17

*Notice to whom one finally appeals [in Matt. 18:15–17]. What court has the final word? It is not a bishop, a pope, or a presbytery; it is not an assembly, a synod, a convention, or a conference. It is not even a pastor or a board of elders, a board of deacons or a church committee. It is, quite simply, the church—that is, the assembly of those individual believers who are the church.*
—Mark Dever, *Nine Marks of a Healthy Church*

In this book, we have been carefully "peeling the onion" of spiritual abuse in order to determine its *etiology* or root cause. Readers who insist at this point that the root cause is polity (how a church governs itself) have unfortunately failed to peel the onion to its core. Polity is not the root of the problem—at the core of the onion is the misuse and abuse of *authority*.

It's understandable why one might think that polity is at the root of the problem since polity is the *application* of authority. Different concepts of authority get expressed in different forms of church government. A car does not receive a violation for speeding—the driver does. Likewise, a church government structure is only doing what the church's concept of authority says it should be doing. Polity is just a vehicle for the expression of authority.

For example, if a church believes that one individual has ultimate, unquestionable spiritual authority over everyone else in the church, then it would practice an *episcopal* form of polity found in Anglican, Lutheran, Orthodox, and Roman Catholic churches. If, on the other hand, a church believes that no member exercises authority over others and that only the collective membership of a church exercises authority, then it would practice a *congregational* form of polity. These are just two forms of polity; there are many different types.

Until we understand that *authority informs polity*, we will be inclined to believe that the solution to spiritual abuse lies in simply changing a local church's bylaws or constitution. While those changes may be eventually necessary, they do not address the fundamental issue. Because authority and polity are inextricably linked, a proper understanding of authority is tremendously important if we are to promote and preserve the unity of the faith and successfully cultivate Christ's love in our congregations.

I submit to you that the way a congregation applies its understanding of authority, expressed in the daily function and activities of church life, is a witness of Christ to a watching world. Jesus reflects this truth beautifully when He prays that His disciples "may all be one, just as you, Father, are in me, and I in you, that they also may be in us, so that the world may believe that you have sent me."[63] It is sobering to realize that the manifestation of a congregation's unity has an evangelistic purpose—to show unbelievers that God indeed exists and that He loves them with an everlasting love and has sent His Son so they might know Him.

Biblical polity also provides the means or structure by which church members enjoy the love, protection, and justice of Christ as it is expressed through the body of Christ. In his book *The Church and the Surprising Offense of God's Love*, Jonathan Leeman stresses how polity has the capacity to ultimately affirm or undermine the reality of the Gospel:

> Most evangelicals have pushed the question of church structure into the category of nonessential and therefore of non-importance. The gospel is important, even essential, we say. Church structure is neither. And since questions of church structure only divide Christians…it's best to leave it out of the conversation altogether. Right?

---
[63] John 17:21

> What if that's wrong? What if God in His wisdom, actually revealed both content and form, both a message and a medium, both a gospel and a polity, perfectly suited to one another? Couldn't pushing questions of church structure into the category of 'what respectable evangelicals shouldn't hold strong opinions about' eventually undermine the gospel itself?[64]

While I agree with Leeman, it seems the problem of polity continues to be thought of as *the sole cause* for the proclivity of spiritual abuse experienced by many in the body of Christ. To blame polity for abuse *seems* plausible since polity likely does have some effect on the overall health or dysfunction of a congregation, but all too often, it is used as a convenient scapegoat on which to place the blame for many of the atrocities related to spiritual abuse. As we noted above, authority *informs* polity, so the real culprit of spiritual abuse remains unnoticed by most of the church—the misuse and abuse of *authority*, exercised primarily by leaders in the church and enabled by passive congregations. Remember, polity is simply the vehicle that carries the passenger of authority—that passenger can be malevolent (an abusive use of authority) or a friend (a proper use of biblical authority). Changing a sentence or two of the church bylaws will only provide a temporary solution. A bad driver with a better car is still a bad driver. It's also not uncommon for authoritarian leaders to promise changes in polity as a means of pla-

---

[64] Jonathan Leeman, *The Church and the Surprising Offense of God's Love* (Wheaton, IL: Crossway, 2010), 17.

cating the flock, and undiscerning church members will often perceive this as evidence of genuine reform. In reality, though, these leaders rarely have any intention of relinquishing control or changing the way authority is exercised in the church.

Jesus made it very clear—He does not want any member of His body, particularly leaders, to have authority over others in a hierarchical or controlling way; for when someone has authority and/or control over you, he has power to manipulate and abuse you. Jesus made certain that those who have the privilege of leading in the church understood that their leadership in the body of Christ was inextricably rooted in *serving* others—not in wielding power, control, or spiritual status over them:

> You know that the rulers of the Gentiles lord it over them, and their great ones exercise authority over them. It shall not be so among you. But whoever would be great among you must be your servant, and whoever would be first among you must be your slave, even as the Son of Man came not to be served but to serve, and to give his life as a ransom for many. (Matt. 20:25–28)

Unfortunately, disregarding this simple biblical principle of servant leadership has caused a lot of pain and suffering throughout the body of Christ. It's why many Christians have been spiritually abused by authoritarian leaders and, as a result, have become disillusioned and discouraged in their Christian walk. Some no longer want anything to do with church or God.

It's incredibly irresponsible that discussions of authority and polity are often completely absent from the diet of the church. When was the last time you heard a sermon preached on these topics? Neither subject really gets very much pulpit time, yet the misuse and abuse of authority is *the root cause for spiritual harm* in the church—and often responsible for the eventual demise of entire congregations!

Therefore, it behooves every responsible member in the body of Christ to make a concerted effort to diligently study Scripture, especially on the subject of authority. In doing so, we guard ourselves against falling prey to the harsh consequences of lending our ears to those who use their authority to control the flock rather than to feed the flock. Again, one's understanding of authority will inevitably inform one's polity, and proper church polity promotes spiritual health among every member of our congregations. This, in turn, creates a compelling witness to our communities. Remember, polity is the *vehicle* by which authority is expressed.

After leaving my own abusive church, I found opportunities to help other believers stuck in similar churches consider more carefully the various terms being used by their leaders to legitimize bad polity. These leaders insisted their polity was orthodox and normative, but this was not the case. I wrote an open letter to one of these churches desperately urging them to become knowledgeable regarding (1) issues pertinent to authority in the church, (2) nuances of terminology that can be misleading, and (3) the problematic form(s) of church government that can result when authority is misapplied. As I close this chapter, I find it appropriate to include this letter here in full.

# THE URIAH SYNDROME

Dear brothers and sisters,

In most cases where a plurality of elders is mentioned in the context of church government, it is usually assumed that the congregation has some meaningful involvement in how those elders are chosen and whether or not there is biblical warrant to remove them if necessary. Nearly all evangelical theologians, including Grudem and Erickson, understand "elder-led churches" to be *congregational-elder-led churches* and not simply *ruled by elders*. In my opinion, SGM is a hierarchical, top-down form of church government that resembles a papacy or episcopal system more than any other form of polity. This is not so much a criticism as it is a point of fact. In my opinion, SGM polity is in direct opposition to the admonition of Jesus when He said:

"You know that the rulers of the Gentiles lord it over them, and their great ones exercise authority over them. It shall not be so among you. But whoever would be great among you must be your servant" (Matt. 20:25–26).

We, as a church, fail grievously when we abdicate our responsibility to be our brother's keeper when one of our members is publicly and/or wrongfully castigated or harmed, and resolution is not forthcoming.

A church is biblically irresponsible if its members do not raise their voices on behalf of one another. They cannot say, "It's not our responsibility. We are an elder-led church. The elders know best, and they will take care of it." On the contrary, when the elders in an elder-led church foul something up, it is the church's responsibility to say and do something about it.

Brothers and sisters, this arrangement (having leaders who are not members of the local congregation make ultimate decisions for the church) violates the *autonomy of the local church*, a concept that was gained through the blood, sweat, and tears of the Reformation. It subverts the biblical authority of the local church along with its inherent right and responsibility to govern itself, and it's a misapplication of the biblical relationship between the body of Christ and those who have the privilege and responsibility to lead the *local church*.

It must be understood that SGM polity stands isolated in the larger evangelical church. "Elder-led" has a completely different meaning and application in other evangelical, reformed churches. The term "elder-led," as used by SGM, is misleading because its normative and accepted meaning is fundamentally different when used by SGM.

Contrary to what you might think, I believe we have a responsibility, as the body of Christ, to exercise our God-given authority in the local church where the Holy Spirit has placed us. This includes monitoring ourselves and those who preach and teach, exercising church discipline when necessary, and being our brother's keeper.

However, *we in SGM have been systematically taught the church has absolutely no authority whatsoever.* This is exactly why many of the maladies throughout our history have occurred. The church has been asleep at the wheel. We have abdicated our biblical responsibility. We must repent of this nonsense! We are responsible for one another. We are our brother's keeper. When something is amiss in our local body, it is *ultimately* the responsibility of all church members, collectively, to ensure things are made right. When a local church fails to do this, it has lost its moorings, and shipwreck is sure to follow. As John Piper reminds us,

Under Christ and his word, the final court of appeal in the local church in deciding matters of disagreement is the congregation itself. (This is implied, first, in the fact that the leaders are not to lead by coercion but by persuasion and free consent [1 Peter 5:3]; second, in the fact that elders may be censured [1 Timothy 5:19]; and third, in the fact that in Matthew 18:15–20 the church is the final court of appeal in matters of discipline).[65]

In the final analysis, we must not point our finger at those in leadership as the source and blame for our problems. We must turn our finger around and point it at ourselves (collectively as the church) because that is where God points it. As has been stated so well, "The church has been given the keys." The keys (ultimate authority in the church) have not been given to the pope, a synod, committee, or group of individuals, regardless of their leadership title or position. The keys have been given to the body of Christ!

---

[65] John Piper, "Rethinking the Governance Structure at Bethlehem Baptist Church," Desiring God, last modified April 27, 2000, https://www.desiringgod.org/articles/rethinking-the-governance-structure-at-bethlehem-baptist-church.

# Study Notes

# 8

# THEOLOGY IS NOT THE PROBLEM

*Then Jesus said to the crowds and to his disciples, "The scribes and the Pharisees sit on Moses' seat, so do and observe whatever they tell you, but not the works they do. For they preach, but do not practice.*
—Matthew 23:1–3

*The responsibility of maintaining true doctrine and practice is directed toward the entire church. This is not to say that those elected by the church do not in a special sense bear this obligation. But the final obligation rests with the church.*
—Robert Saucy, *The Church in God's Program*

Just as some Christians believe the etiology of spiritual abuse is rooted in unhealthy forms of church polity, others believe its root cause is poor *theology*. After all, a church that holds to unorthodox doctrine is likely a breeding ground for spiritual harm. However, a church that teaches orthodox doctrine and preaches a biblically informed Gospel message can still remain in error because of how it *practices* those doctrines. Poor methodology (practice) negates good theology (teaching).

This is precisely the problem Jesus warned about in Matthew 23:1–3, cited above. He *affirmed* the theology of the scribes and Pharisees ("observe whatever they tell you") but took issue with their practice ("[don't do] the works they do") because it ultimately revealed their blatant and destructive hypocrisy ("they preach, but do not practice"). Jesus did not take kindly to hypocrisy, particularly from leaders.

> Woe to you, scribes and Pharisees, hypocrites! For you are like whitewashed tombs, which outwardly appear beautiful, but within are full of dead people's bones and all uncleanness. So you also outwardly appear righteous to others, but within you are full of hypocrisy and lawlessness. (Matt. 23:27–28)
>
> You load people with burdens hard to bear, and you yourselves do not touch the burdens with one of your fingers. (Luke 11:46)

This familiar principle of "practicing what we preach" serves as a reminder that our methodology (our motivations, behavior, and practice) must correspond to sound theology (what we preach and teach), lest we be found guilty of the same error as the Pharisees: *hypocrisy*. Therefore, it behooves congregations to keep this principle in mind as they listen to and observe both the theology taught from the pulpit and the methodology that results from its implementation. Any discrepancy between the two is a cause for concern and reason to hold both as suspect and potentially problematic. Incongruence between theology and practice is likely to produce a toxic culture of legalism, performance-based acceptance, and conditional love.

Discrepancies between a Christian organization's teaching and practice also leaves it open to the charge of being a cult. The definitive proof of a group's being a cult is not necessarily in what the group *says* as much as what it *does*; this is why it is so difficult to convince people involved in Christian cults that something is wrong. Cults are ultimately defined by their *methodology*, not their theology. That's why those who defend a Christian cult will first point to the theology of the group—which often passes as orthodox and mainstream. Even seasoned evangelical leaders have been duped by abusive leaders who teach sound biblical doctrine but are unaware of (or choose to ignore) the "bleating of sheep" who have been sorely abused by theologically correct leaders. The fact that no one would typically choose to find oneself in this kind of situation demonstrates the subtle power and influence of deceptive teaching from misguided leaders. The kind of theology and methodology they propagate is often more associated with Satan than God. That's why Paul, in the book of Galatians, contends passionately for *grace* and warns about the dangers of embracing a different Gospel than the one he taught.

> I am astonished that you are so quickly deserting him who called you in the grace of Christ and are turning to a different gospel—not that there is another one, but there are some who trouble you and want to distort the gos-

pel of Christ. But even if we or an angel from heaven should preach to you a gospel contrary to the one we preached to you, let him be accursed. As we have said before, so now I say again: If anyone is preaching to you a gospel contrary to the one you received, let him be accursed…O foolish Galatians! Who has bewitched you?" (Gal. 1:6-9; 3:1)

We should be sobered by Paul's appeal as he pleads for us to remain faithful to sound biblical teaching. His choice of words, like *bewitched* and *accursed*, reflect God's righteous indignation at a perversion of Scripture which can lead to toxic methodologies like fear, threats, blackmail, coercion, manipulation, condemnation, and emotional withdrawal. Some of these are conspicuous and obviously wrong, like blackmail, threats, and coercion, but most are subtle and almost imperceptible, like fear, manipulation, condemnation, and emotional withdrawal. Other common examples of toxic methodologies include:[66]

# Deception

- Deliberately holding back information
- Distorting information to make it acceptable
- Outright lying

---

[66] SGM Survivors, post by "Unassimilated," accessed December 11, 2010, http://www.sgmsurvivors.com/2010/12/11.

## Minimizing/Discouraging Access to Alternative Sources of Information

— For example, books, articles, newspapers, magazines, TV, radio, former members

## Keeping Members So Busy That They Don't Have Time to Think for Themselves

— Pressure and expectation to attend multiple mandatory meetings, conferences, seminars, and workshops

## Compartmentalizing Information or Having "Outsider" / "Insider" Doctrines

— Information not kept freely accessible
— Information varies at different levels within a pyramid structure
— Leadership decides who "needs to know" what

## Spying on Others

— Pairing members up in a "buddy system" to monitor and control others
— Reporting deviant thoughts, feelings, and actions to leadership

## Unethical Use of Confession

- Information about "sins" used to abolish identity boundaries
- Past "sins" used to manipulate and control, no forgiveness or absolution

## Extensive Use of Cult-Generated Information and Propaganda

- For example, newsletters, magazines, journals, audiotapes, videotapes, etc.
- Statements from noncult sources taken out of context and misquoted

These toxic methodologies do the most harm when they are assimilated into the culture of the church, which ensures further abuse from leaders and from the deceived congregants who have absorbed these destructive methodologies. This presents a puzzling irony in that the members of the church become the very ones who enable and propagate their own demise, misfortune, and abuse by tolerating such behavior by leaders.

One couple I know had been shunned from their church and pronounced "divisive" by the leadership simply because they had expressed legitimate concerns about some of the scriptures their leaders used to justify removing one pastor and installing another. While talking with the leadership about this issue, the couple felt perpetually backed into a corner and intimidated. Their leaders questioned the couple's motives and quoted verse after verse from the Bible in an effort to justify their authority to make unilateral decisions divorced from any consideration by those in the church. In fact, because the church had fallen prey to the dynamic discussed in the previous paragraph, the entire church wholeheartedly supported the leadership's position and thereby exacerbated the harm done to this couple.

Today, many reform-minded Christians are making tireless efforts to align their churches with biblical doctrine and practice in order to prevent or remove legalistic and authoritarian leadership. Unfortunately, they often become frustrated and exasperated as they attempt to navigate the waters of reform because leaders who ascribe to this type of hierarchical, top-down church structure tend to obfuscate any efforts that could threaten their loss of power and control over the congregation. They will assure prospective reformers that making a few revisions in the church bylaws or constitution will easily rectify the problem. In reality, this is rarely a solution. Rather, this response is meant to give the *appearance* that meaningful change is sure to come.

To illustrate this point, I've included a document[67] from the leaders of an SGM congregation that was written to change the church's existing polity in order to appease the congregation who had serious concerns about the behavior of these leaders. At first glance, the proposal seems to reflect an orthodox, traditional, and acceptable theological position on ecclesiology (the doctrine of the church) and its application to church governance. Unfortunately, closer scrutiny reveals no truly substantial changes had been proposed. Note the paper's

---

[67] "Covenant Life Polity Position Paper," *Reformed Churchmen* (blog), July 14, 2012, http://reformationanglicanism.blogspot.com/2012/07/sgm-saga-covenant-life-polity-position.html.

ing of a church and, by affirmation of elders, actually exercises them.

*If this means that elders must affirm each member's power, gift, and/or calling, then this again reveals spiritual arrogance on the part of the leaders and is definitely false.*

Any theory which speaks of the appointment of rulers except by the free acts of the local church is in error.

*True.*

In this biblical model of authority, Christ alone, as head of the church, prescribes the need for rulers and graciously provides elders to rule and oversee His church.

*Misleading. How does God "graciously provide elders to rule and oversee His church" in this view? Through SGM's Book of Church Order, of course, in which other elders make this decision (or "provision") for the church. Shepherding, watching over, and caring for the flock of God is emphasized more often than ruling in Scripture. Why emphasize ruling? This arrangement conveniently ensures that the congregation has absolutely no authority or power over leaders.*

But it is the local church, working with its leaders, that affirms its officers.

*Why make a distinction between the "local church" and "its leaders" when simply using the term* local church *would suffice? The local church, by nature, contains within itself its own leaders.*

These elders are to be called by God (Ephesians 4:11),

*How are elders called by God? Scripture does teach that elders may be called by God; however, practically speaking, they are first chosen by the church, not by other leaders or elders apart from the church.*

qualified according to Scripture (1 Timothy 3:1–7), and examined and installed by the church.

*Acts 1 and 6 demonstrate that elders, pastors, and deacons are actually appointed by other elders after the church has chosen them. The church collectively prays for and installs leaders.*

The stewardship of shepherding the flock of God has been given to the elders, as they are undershepherds of the Chief Shepherd, Jesus Christ. Elders are to exercise this God-given authority in the church as servants, not lording it over the sheep (Mark 10:42–45).

*The only authority elders, pastors, leaders have is declarative authority: the authority to preach/teach God's Word. They do not have effectual authority to violate anyone's will or cause any member to do anything. Only the church has both declarative and effectual authority.*

Such authority is ministerial, spiritual, and declarative.

*True, leaders have declarative authority, but they absolutely do not have spiritual authority over anyone. I'm not sure what "ministerial authority" means. If it means to carry out activities such as preaching, teaching, officiating weddings and funerals, and conducting the daily business of the church, then this seems reasonable. However, major decisions affecting the church must always first be vetted by the congregation. Leaders must always be mindful that they serve at the pleasure of the church and never in a dictatorial or totalitarian fashion. Their job is to facilitate and execute the agenda of the church, not their own.*

As clearly revealed by the Chief Shepherd, there can be no lording, domination, or pre-eminence of power in the church.

*True! So why does most of the content of this paper seem to argue for leaders having a special and unique authority over the congregation, particularly to rule?*

Did you notice the sleight of hand in the above paper and the seemingly innocuous word choices the author of this paper uses in order to convey the ultimate message that elders and leaders are *rulers* who have authority over everyone else in the church? This method is typical of leaders and organizations who insist on maintaining control, authority, and power over individual church members and, by extension, the entire congregation. It is an unfortunate example of the "Galatian error" (legalism and lording over) and has no biblical support whatsoever. Of course, these leaders would flatly deny that gaining control or power was their intention or motive. Whether in the pulpit or through the drafting of new bylaws and church constitutions, controlling leaders will make every effort to use language that appears at first to be theologically correct but, in practice, proves otherwise.

As mentioned earlier in this book, a sure test that reveals a leader's position on authority is to simply ask him, "Does the church have authority?"

If *yes*, ask for examples where the church exercises that authority.

If *no*, ask how the leader reconciles his answer with all the biblical examples of the church exercising authority found later in this book.

Then ask the leader what Jesus meant when He said, "You know that those who are considered rulers of the Gentiles lord it over them, and their great ones exercise authority over them. *It shall not be so among you* [emphasis mine]. But whoever would be great among you must be your servant" (Mark 10:42–43).

Finally, ask the leader what the function of leadership is as described in Matthew 18:15–20.

In recent years, several prominent leaders in the Christian community have supported and endorsed the ministry of spiritually abusive pastors and groups plagued with authoritarian leadership practices, spiritual abuse, and other scandalous problems—despite clear evidence of these issues being systemic to these individuals and organizations. Instead of being encouraged to return to their flocks to diligently pursue accountability, repentance, and/or reconciliation (per Matthew 18 and Titus 2), they are coddled, defended, and invited to speak at large conferences and/or sit as board members in various parachurch organizations.

*The first statement is True, "Church power belongs essentially to the whole body of believers, whether officers or not." The second statement is False: Rather, the entire church is endued with the power of God. Each member manifests the power of the Holy Spirit through various gifts and callings. God's power is not exclusive to its officers (1 Cor. 12).*

The primary depository or subject of church power is not in the office-bearers exclusively...

*True.*

...nor the whole body of believers exclusively...

*False. The whole body of believers certainly would include the officers and/or elders, would it not? Why make this distinction? This is very telling regarding how the leaders perceive themselves spiritually compared to laypeople. There is no hierarchy in the body of Christ (1 Cor. 12:12–26).*

...but in both working together as an organic whole.

*True.*

This principle rules out strict congregationalism as well as strict prelacy (Matthew 18, Galatians 3).

*False. It affirms strict congregationalism and rules out strict prelacy.*

The people of God in a local church possess the combined powers, gifts, and call-

subtle phrasing and deviation from biblical principles, which ultimately nullified the idea of laypeople having any substantive voice, power, or authority. The leaders, on the other hand, continued to maintain authority, power, and control over the affairs of the congregation.

My comments below are indented and italicized.

### Polity Position Paper

>Authority in the church can properly be said to be *in actu primo* (actual or real authority) to the whole church itself and *in actusecundo* (the function or exercise of authority) to those especially called, namely the elders.
>
>*False. Both the Bible and orthodox, historic Christian doctrine affirm that the function or exercise of authority is the responsibility of the entire church. Perhaps the most poignant example of this is found in Matthew 18:15–20, which does not once mention leaders, elders, pastors, or bishops but clearly identifies the church as the final court of appeal and the only entity authorized to effectually remove someone from the church. Though they may think so, leaders do not have such authority. For them to presume so is to ignore the clear teaching of Scripture.*
>
>Church power belongs essentially to the whole body of believers, whether officers or not. To state it concisely, the power of the church is vested by God to the body and then exercised through its officers.

The Christian leaders who support these abusive individuals and groups appear to restrict themselves to appraising only their theology and doctrine while completely disregarding the toxic culture produced by their harmful practice and methodology. They argue that necessary and adequate reforms have been drafted and implemented through the introduction of new and improved bylaws, like the example given above, and therefore are convinced these abusive organizations have satisfied their scrutiny. Meanwhile, little to no attention is given to those who argue that abuse continues to occur. This leaves many in the church to echo the prophet Samuel: "What then is this bleating of the sheep in my ears and the lowing of the oxen that I hear?"[68] In some cases, thousands of congregants have raised their voices against glaring injustices committed against their children, fellow congregants, and associate pastors—all to no avail. The following anonymous writer reflects the precarious spiritual position in which these congregants find themselves when they continue to ignore what we have discussed thus far in this chapter.

> I have felt a renewed urgency to warn those who remain in a SGM church that you are placing yourself and your family in a very precarious and dangerous situation. I appeal to you to judge SGM according to the measure Scripture encourages, particularly regarding the *actions/fruit* of those proclaiming to be caring for God's people…You must make a distinction between theology

---

[68] 1 Samuel 15:14

and methodology. While a plausible case might be made regarding SGM's theology, the practice, application, or methodology of that theology has resulted in serious spiritual, psychological, and emotional harm to many of our brothers and sisters throughout SGM churches. SGM's spiritual abuse of many of its members is *systemic*, despite assertions by SGM leadership to the contrary.

As mentioned previously, several leaders even deserted their congregations when such concerns were raised instead of making a concerted effort at reconciliation and repentance where necessary. This error of judgement occurs when leaders are evaluated based on what they *say* rather than what they *do*. They preach but do not practice.

But how can right preaching and wrong practice even coexist within a congregation? How can sound theology be congruent with spiritually abusive methodology? As I've said before, abusive leaders want to possess absolute power and control over their congregations. This, for them, is their holy grail. In order to appease this lust for power and control, they must convince their followers that the Bible *authorizes* them to have that kind of control. This is also the key ingredient that defines a cult: *deception*. When leaders succeed at convincing their congregations that God, through His inerrant Word, has mandated leaders to have control over their churches, a personality cult often forms in which leaders refuse to be held accountable by congregants, and congregants abdicate their duty to hold leaders accountable. These leaders demonstrate spiritual arrogance, pride, and self-exaltation, which inevitably lead to all manner of harm. Every member of the congregation must become biblically literate and demonstrate a commitment to challenge dubious teaching and methodology whenever it occurs. Paul provides us an excellent example of this principle at work when it became necessary to challenge Peter:

> In the book of Galatians, even the apostle Peter made a mistake and had to be corrected by the apostle Paul. Nobody then is above challenge. Systems of church governance which give mechanisms to hold senior leaders accountable to their followers help correct such personality cults developing. If your church doesn't have those, seriously consider pushing for reform or moving to a church with healthier governance.[69]

In closing, I trust you have seen that it is not enough for us as Christians to merely *say* the right things and *believe* the right doctrines—we must also be willing and able to *do* them. We need to practice what we preach, and we need to pay attention to whether others practice what they preach, particularly where leadership is concerned. We should also be suspicious of theology that is not accompanied by sound methodology. Good theology, constitutions, and bylaws alone do not make a healthy church. In order to distinguish authentic biblical Christianity

---

[69] Philip Rosenthal, "How Bible Preachers Can Turn Into Cult Leaders," The Aquila Report, September 4, 2012, http://theaquilareport.com/how-bible-preachers-can-turn-into-cult-leaders/.

from a Christian sect, a cult, or an unhealthy church, we should be making comprehensive assessments of both theology (teaching) *and* methodology (motivation, behavior, and practice). Only then will we be able to discern whether or not a church is healthy and producing fruit that is safe for spiritual consumption, as Scripture instructs:

> Beware of false prophets, who come to you in sheep's clothing but inwardly are ravenous wolves. You will recognize them by their fruits. Are grapes gathered from thorn bushes, or figs from thistles? So, every healthy tree bears good fruit, but the diseased tree bears bad fruit. A healthy tree cannot bear bad fruit, nor can a diseased tree bear good fruit. Every tree that does not bear good fruit is cut down and thrown into the fire. Thus you will recognize them by their fruits. (Matt. 7:15–20)

Because of their prominent and influential position in many congregations today, leaders can often be the catalyst for systemic problems when they misuse and abuse authority in the church. However, the Bible does affirm a certain type of authority that leaders *are* authorized to have and expected to exercise. In fact, as we will see in the next chapter, the health and welfare of every church member—including the leaders themselves—depends on a proper understanding and expression of that authority.

# Study Notes

# 9

# THE AUTHORITY OF LEADERS

*This is how one should regard us, as servants of Christ and stewards of the mysteries of God.*
　　　　　　　　　　　　—1 Corinthians 4:1

*The first sign of an abusive group is that it is authoritarian. When it comes right down to it, control is more important than personal spiritual welfare. Leaders in an authoritarian system are not teachable.*
　　　　—David Henke, Watchman Fellowship

*The Church does not need brilliant personalities but faithful servants of Jesus and the brethren. Not in the former but in the latter is the lack.*
　　　　—Dietrich Bonhoeffer, Life Together

Your theological position on the *authority of leaders* is one of the most important spiritual issues to settle as a Christian and is worthy of your diligent and arduous study due to the profound repercussions it will have in both your personal life and the life of your local church.

For example, you may believe that Jesus authorizes special and gifted individuals to exercise authority over others in the body of Christ. If so, you will likely subscribe to an episcopal form of polity. As noted previously, this is a hierarchical system of church government, which is found in the Roman Catholic Church, as well as in some Protestant evangelical churches that have leadership positions of "senior pastor" or "lead elder." In this top-down authority structure of leaders and laypeople, church matters are exclusively decided upon by leaders who occupy lofty positions of power. They typically determine who else will lead the church, what their salary will be, if and when they will be fired, how finances are managed, and anything else regarding the day-to-day activities and responsibilities of the church. At times, the exercise of such control and authority is obvious, like when leadership simply informs the congregation who their new leaders, deacons, or elders will be. Other times, it can be subtle, like when leadership teaches the congregation to submit to and obey whatever they say, at the risk of experiencing their displeasure and, by extension, the displeasure of God. In either case, the message is the same: leaders have the power, and laypeople must obey them. What enables leaders to function in this authoritative capacity is the congregation's concession of its own autonomy and volition in which laypeople, at the risk of being rebuked and shunned, demonstrate unquestioned obedience to their leaders' instruction.

Fortunately, this is not the view of authority held by Scripture. The Bible affirms the doctrine of the priesthood of *all* believers, in which each church member enjoys his own personal relationship with God as a holy and royal priest (1 Peter 2:5, 9). We will discuss this topic more fully in the next chapter. Suffice it to say, on this view, every congregant operates as an equal, interdependent member of the body of Christ with gifts to benefit the others. No member is considered separate from the congregation, higher or lower in position or value, or more or less gifted than any other member. We can see this view expressed in the following passages:

> That there may be no division in the body, but that the members may have the same care for one another. If one member suffers, all suffer together; if one member is honored, all rejoice together. (1 Cor. 12:25–26)
>
> For as in one body we have many members, and the members do not all have the same function, so we, though many, are one body in Christ, and individually members one of another. (Rom. 12:4–5)
>
> There is one body and one Spirit—just as you were called to the one hope that belongs to your call— one Lord, one faith, one baptism, one God and Father of all, who is over all and through all and in all. But grace was given to each one of us according to the measure of Christ's gift. (Eph. 4:4–7)
>
> Rather, speaking the truth in love, we are to grow up in every way into him who is the head, into Christ, from whom the whole body, joined and held together by every joint

with which it is equipped, when each part is working properly, makes the body grow so that it builds itself up in love. (Eph. 4:15–16)

## The Function and Disposition of Leadership

In Mark 10:35–45, Jesus gives some of his most pointed admonitions in Scripture. Here, he explains His expectations for both the *function* (the operation or behavior) and *disposition* (the attitude or demeanor) of leadership in the church.

> James and John, the sons of Zebedee, came up to [Jesus] and said to him, "Teacher, we want you to do for us whatever we ask of you." And he said to them, "What do you want me to do for you?" And they said to him, "Grant us to sit, one at your right hand and one at your left, in your glory." Jesus said to them, "You do not know what you are asking. Are you able to drink the cup that I drink, or to be baptized with the baptism with which I am baptized?" And they said to him, "We are able." And Jesus said to them, "The cup that I drink you will drink, and with the baptism with which I am baptized, you will be baptized, but to sit at my right hand or at my left is not mine to grant, but it is for those for whom it has been prepared." And when the ten heard it, they began to be indignant at James and John. And Jesus called

them to him and said to them, "You know that those who are considered rulers of the Gentiles lord it over them, and their great ones exercise authority over them. *But it shall not be so among you* [emphasis mine]. But whoever would be great among you must be your servant, and whoever would be first among you must be slave of all. For even the Son of Man came not to be served but to serve, and to give his life as a ransom for many."

First, let's start with the *function* of leadership. In the above passage, Jesus emphatically prohibits leaders from functioning in a top-down, hierarchical form of authority. To make His point clear, He references a type of leadership that was evidently very familiar to His disciples, saying, "*You know* that those who are considered rulers of the Gentiles lord it over them, and their great ones exercise authority over them. *But it shall not be so among you* [emphases mine]." It is critical that we recognize Jesus's unequivocal prohibition of this secular authority structure being applied to the governance of the church. Jesus is clear: there will be *no* top-down, hierarchical authority structure in which leaders hold authority over others in the congregation.

The apostle Paul later reiterated this principle through instruction and practice as he ministered to the church in Corinth: "Not that we lord it over your faith, but we work with you for your joy, for you stand firm in your faith" (2 Cor. 1:24). Others who have held the privilege and responsibility of leading and caring for God's people similarly follow this principle throughout the New Testament. They recognized that *lording over* or *exercising authority over* others was not characteristic of good leadership in the church. While it might be found in civil government, the military, or business, Jesus said a hierarchical model of leadership would have no place within His church. As Edmund Clowney says,

> The undershepherd is not a stand-in for the Lord. He presents the word of the Lord, not his own decree; he enforces the revealed will of the Lord, not his own wishes. For that reason, any undermining of the authority of Scripture turns church government into spiritual tyranny. If church governors add to or subtract from the word of God, they make themselves lords over the consciences of others.[70]

Second, Jesus addresses the *disposition*—the demeanor or attitude—leaders are to exhibit as they interact with individual members and the congregation as a whole. They are to function as *servants*, embracing the example of Christ, remembering that even the Son of Man came not to be served but to serve others. They should not dictate, manipulate, insist, coerce, or demand, but instead should be servants of all. Unfortunately, this biblical job description is being increasingly disregarded by those who hold the privileged responsibility of shepherding the people of God.

---

[70] Edmund Clowney, *The Message of 1 Peter* (Downers Grove, IL: InterVarsity, 1984), 202.

Jesus also gives a profound demonstration of the *humility* He expects from leaders when He calls a child over to the disciples—the leaders—and says, "Truly, I say to you, unless you turn and become like children, you will never enter the kingdom of heaven. Whoever humbles himself like this child is the greatest in the kingdom of heaven" (Matt. 18:2–4). The apostle Paul elaborates on this expectation of humility during his exhortation to the church at Philippi:

> Have this mind among yourselves, which is yours in Christ Jesus, who, though he was in the form of God, did not count equality with God a thing to be grasped, but emptied himself, by taking the form of a servant, being born in the likeness of men. And being found in human form, he humbled himself by becoming obedient to the point of death, even death on a cross. (Phil. 2:5–8)

Throughout the New Testament, we see examples of leaders emulating Christ in both *function* (as servants) and *disposition* (with humility). By contrast, leaders who function by exercising authority over others tend to develop a selfish and proud disposition:

> Lording it over the flock provokes church fights and splits. A domineering spirit in elders provokes mature men of strong minds and independent judgment to leave the church. These very ones would have

the greatest potential for future leadership in the assembly. Dictatorial measures make lesser men craven and dependent, stunting their true growth. But it also has its harmful effects on the "lords over God's heritage." It makes them egotistical and self serving.[71]

## Declarative vs. Effectual Authority

In order to understand what proper biblical authority is, we need to first specify what the nature of the authority is that Scripture authorizes leaders to have. To do that, we need to distinguish between *declarative* and *effectual* authority. This may sound a little complicated, but if we fail to make this distinction, we will misunderstand biblical leadership—to our own detriment.

First, let's talk about *declarative* authority. This is the authority that *leaders* have to declare the truths of Scripture. This means that our obedience and submission to leaders is *conditional* upon whether or not those leaders *are* actually declaring the truth of Scripture. If they are, then we ought to submit and obey them because in doing so, we are ultimately submitting to the authority of Scripture. For this reason, all Christians are authorized and expected to exercise declarative authority, not just leaders! In our interactions with other believers, especially with regard to difficult problems and decisions, our views should reflect what the Bible says and not our own opinions or preferences. However, if leaders are declaring something non-

---

[71] Walter J. Chantry, "The Christian Ministry and Self Denial," *Banner of Truth Magazine*, November 1979, 23.

biblical or extrabiblical, then we are *not* obligated to listen to or obey such teaching. Scripture prohibits leaders from using the pulpit to advance their own agendas, touting their opinions as "gospel truth," or instructing, teaching, and proclaiming anything other than what can be substantiated by the Word of God. The church is meant to submit to and obey leaders as a response to the truths of Scripture—not to the whims, desires, and preferences of whoever is preaching. This is because leaders are supposed to be serving not their own will but the will of God, as pastor Samuel Miller points out:

> The authority of Church officers is not original, but *subordinate and delegated*: that is, as they are his *servants*, and act under his commission, and in his name, they have power only to *declare* what the Scriptures reveal as his will, and to pronounce sentence accordingly. If they attempt to establish any other terms of communion than those which his word warrants; or to undertake to exercise authority in a manner which He has not authorized, they incur guilt, and have no right to exact obedience [emphases mine].[72]

Unfortunately, this simple but profound biblical principle is seldom taught by leaders or even considered by those in the congregation. *Unconditional* submission and obedience by the congregation appears to be the norm in many evan-

---

[72] Samuel Miller, *An Essay on the Warrant, Nature, and Duties of the Office of the Ruling Elder* (Philadelphia: Presbyterian Board of Education, 1832), 15.

gelical churches today. This, in turn, produces impotent and anemic churches that lack the confidence to live out the high and robust nature of their calling as "the pillar and foundation of truth." Moreover, the expectation that church leaders require unconditional submission actually challenges the role of Christ as the sole spiritual mediator between God and man, as professor Ron Enroth explains,

> In the face of increasing dependence on strong leadership in Christian circles, evangelicals who value the legitimate role of biblical submission and headship must reaffirm the freedom which characterizes the new life in Christ. We must resist any teaching that brings into question Christ's role as the sole mediator (go-between) between God and man. We must reassert that no Christian is ever called upon to give unquestioning obedience to anyone. We ultimately must accept only the lordship of Christ.[73]

Now that we've looked at declarative authority, let us look at *effectual* authority. This kind of authority is given by Jesus and is only exercised by the Church:

> On this rock I will build my church, and the gates of hell shall not prevail against it. I will give you the keys of the kingdom of heaven,

---

[73] Ronald Enroth, "The Power Abusers," Apologetics Index, accessed August 18, 2018, http://www.apologeticsindex.org/a08.html.

and whatever you bind on earth shall be bound in heaven, and whatever you loose on earth shall be loosed in heaven. (Matt. 16:18–19)

Jonathan Leeman, in his excellent book *The Church and the Surprising Offense of God's Love*, elaborates on how *effectual authority* is distinct from *declarative authority*:

> The authority of Matthew 16 is the effectual power to bind and loose on earth, and it's an authority that's to be exercised by the entire church. By "effectual," I mean it achieves what it commands. If the church says that an individual is excluded, he is excluded. Yet neither in this passage or in any other do we see a connection between this organizational charter and the office of elder or overseer.... [Leaders'] authority is not effectual. They cannot command or formally require a member or even the church to do something.... [T]here is no passage in Scripture that tells me that an elder or overseer, one or many, bears the effectual authority of Matthew 16 to bind and loose for disobedience. The church, of course, can. It can unilaterally exclude someone from membership.[74]

---

[74] Jonathan Leeman, *The Surprising Offense of God's Love* (Wheaton, IL: Crossway. 2010), 212–213.

Did you catch the difference? Declarative authority is the authority of all Christians *to declare the truth of Scripture*, whereas effectual authority is the exclusive authority of a local congregation to *effect change in that particular body of believers*. We can see the church exercising effectual authority in choosing new leaders (Acts 1:15–26, 6:2–6), judging disputes (Matt. 18:15–17; 1 Cor. 6:1–3), removing members (1 Cor. 5:1–5), and restoring members (2 Cor. 2:5–8). I encourage you, the reader, to conduct your own Bible study to see how often the church is involved in weighty matters affecting the life of a congregation. I've included appendix 2 at the back of the book as a resource to help in your own personal study.

Again, while all believers have (and are expected to exercise) *declarative* authority, it is only the collective membership of a local church that is authorized to exercise *effectual* authority, which is the authority to actually bring something to pass. To use biblical terms, it is only the church who has been given authority by Christ Himself to "bind" and "loose" on earth (Matt. 18:18–20). Talk of "binding" and "loosing" was common among Jewish rabbis at the time, and biblical scholars agree that the meaning of these expressions is incontestable: *to bind* meant "to forbid," and *to loose* meant "to permit."[75]

Sadly, a large contingent of the church has failed to recognize the important distinction between declarative and effectual authority for nearly three generations, ever since the authoritarian, hierarchical leadership structure of the Shepherding Movement wreaked havoc on vast numbers of believers in the 1970s. Since then, it has negatively influenced *contemporary*

---

[75] Bob DeWaay, "Binding and Loosing: Part 1," *Critical Issues Commentary* 1, no. 1 (1992): 1.

leaders like Mahaney, Driscoll, MacDonald, and anyone else who believes leaders are granted an unbridled mandate to exert authority over everyone else in their churches.

Tragically, even though two of the Shepherding Movement's *own founders* eventually recognized their error, repented, and asked forgiveness from those whom their movement had harmed, many of today's Christian leaders seem unable to recognize the toxicity of the same hierarchical leadership model. As a result, the wounds caused by a myriad of spiritual, emotional, and psychological abuse continue to fester throughout the church. This abuse, caused by the misuse and abuse of authority, goes undetected by many in the church due to a constant diet of teaching and preaching, peppered with admonitions, that encourages the flock to "keep their place" of perpetual subservience to those in leadership. The go-to verse most often cited for such teaching and preaching is, of course, Hebrews 13:17:

> Obey your leaders and submit to them, for they are keeping watch over your souls, as those who will have to give an account. Let them do this with joy and not with groaning, for that would be of no advantage to you.

## Understanding Hebrews 13:17

Seldom has a passage been more misinterpreted and skewed in the effort to justify unquestioned obedience than this one. Without proper exegesis and a diligent study of this passage (and others like it), Christians are prone to being harmed as a result of its misapplication. However, once we understand the difference between *declarative* and *effectual* authority, as well as the meaning of *obey* and *submit*, passages like this one make perfect sense and can be obeyed in earnest.

Unfortunately, authoritarian leaders often teach that Hebrews 13:17 means that church members must *unconditionally* obey and submit to whatever the leaders say, since the leaders will one day give an account to the Lord regarding how well those congregants behaved (obeyed and submitted) while under their authority. As we will see that interpretation is incorrect but it is important to understand *why* it is a faulty interpretation of the text.

In our attempt to be like the Bereans who "received the word with all eagerness, examining the Scriptures daily to see if these things were so," (Acts 17:11) here is Hebrews 13:17 in the original Greek with a short commentary.

> Πείθεσθε τοῖς ἡγουμένοις ὑμῶν καὶ ὑπείκετε, αὐτοὶ γὰρ ἀγρυπνοῦσιν ὑπὲρ τῶν ψυχῶν ὑμῶν ὡς λόγον ἀποδώσοντες, ἵνα μετὰ χαρᾶς τοῦτο ποιῶσιν καὶ μὴ στενάζοντες, ἀλυσιτελὲς γὰρ ὑμῖν τοῦτο.

Πείθεσθε can confidently be used for "obey" (cf. James 3:3). Another translation could be, "Be convinced yourselves with respect to those leading you." ὑπείκετε generally means "listen" or "obey." ἡγουμένοις has a wide range of meanings, as common words generally do. It can stand for "generals," "commanders," and "city rulers."

I've included several volumes in the bibliography to help you understand the complexities of these Greek terms, and the entire Greek New Testament can be read online at: www.nestle-aland.com/en/read-na28-online/

Based on the Greek meaning of the two words in view (*obey* and *submit*), an acceptable paraphrase would be as follows: *Obey* your leaders (allow yourself to be convinced or influenced by the word of God as it is being taught by your leader(s), *submit to them* (have a disposition characterized by a willingness to yield to what is being taught, particularly when a leader appeals for your obedience to God's Word).

Additionally, it is important to note that the command to extend obedience and submission to leaders as they teach the Scriptures is conditional, *not* unconditional. Here are some of the prerequisites and conditions noted in Scripture:

1) The individual who serves as a leader should have first been previously put forward or chosen by the congregation as a possible candidate for leadership/overseer/elder/deacon (Acts 1:23; 6:3–5) as opposed to being unilaterally assigned this position by another leader without the consideration of the congregation—or worse, being unilaterally assigned by someone outside the membership of the congregation.

2) Prior to assuming the responsibilities of leadership, the congregation should have the opportunity to assess the individual's qualifications for leadership using 1 Timothy 3:1–7 and Titus 1:6–9 to evaluate those who aspire to be overseers/elders, and 1 Timothy 3: 8–13 to evaluate those who aspire to be deacons. (The pri-

mary distinction that it is unnecessary to evaluate one's ability to teach if they aspire to the office of deacon.)

3) It is assumed that Hebrews 13:17 refers to *teaching* elders/leaders because the obedience and submission in view presumes that the leader's instruction is informed by the *authority of Scripture* and not by virtue of his title or position. In other words, the congregation is called to obey and submit to *rightly confessing* leaders/teachers as opposed to leaders who speak extra-biblically, espouse their own opinions, or insist on obedience to *preferences* as opposed to clear *biblical principles*. No one should feel compelled to obey or submit to a leader simply by virtue of his title or position (Galatians 1:8,9), but rather because they are proven men of character (1 Timothy 3:1–7; Titus 1:6–9) and teach the Scriptures accurately, rightly dividing the Word of God (2 Timothy 2:15).

4) The entire congregation is obligated to *test* and *weigh* what is taught in an effort to determine its congruency with Scripture (1 John 4:1–3; 1 Tim 1:3–7; 1 Tim 6:3–5; 2 Peter 2:1–3; 1 Thessalonians 5:20,21; Titus 1:10,11; Revelations 2:2).

5) We must remember that while Christ has provided various gifts to the church, one being the gift of teaching (Romans 12:7), we should not ascribe greater authority to an individual based on the gift they might exercise, nor blindly concede obedience by virtue of their job description or title (1 Corinthians 12). Ultimately, we can take heart in Christ's admonition that He is our

*instructor* and as such will help us understand what is taught from the pulpit (Matthew 23:8–12; Luke 12:12).

Lastly, Hebrews 13:17 does not indicate that leaders will give an account for the behavior of *others* in the church. On the contrary, it is a sobering reminder *directed to leaders* that they will one day give an account for how well *they themselves* cared for God's people!

Moreover, our responsibility to obey and submit to leaders is not exclusive to those in leadership but extends to every member in the congregation. This is true because all believers are obligated to respond in submission and obedience to Scripture, regardless of who is speaking to us. However, none of us, including leaders, have the responsibility or authority to cause God's' Word to be *effectual* in another individual's life. This is the exclusive and particular work of the Holy Spirit. Additionally, no congregant or leader is authorized to make a unilateral decision regarding *church discipline*, that is, to impose a sanction upon another except the congregation itself, i.e. excommunication from the congregation or affirmation to the congregation.

It is imperative we understand that, ultimately, only the congregation is authorized by Scripture to evaluate, decide, and impose dispositions of church discipline regarding another congregant (Matthew 18:15–20; 1 Corinthian 5: 1–5; 5:12,13; 2 Corinthians 2:5–11). The pervasive neglect of this biblical principle by many leaders and churches has resulted in unnecessary harm to many a saint and has brought disgrace and disrepute to the name of Christ.

Amazingly, God demonstrates His wisdom, compassion, and protection from frivolous or unwarranted charges for all members of the congregation by manifesting His authority in the *church*. Those from whom He requires obedience and submission regarding leaders have the prerequisite task of choosing, evaluating, and giving their consent accordingly. The benefit of adhering to this biblical precept insures that those who obey and submit to leaders do so having first participated in the vetting, evaluation, and selection of the very ones they are to obey. This is why it is extremely important how congregations go about establishing leadership in the church. The difference is analogous to an arranged marriage, which is forced, devoid of free volition, characterized by external imposition, and primarily based on duty, contrasted with a union that cultivates trust and transparency, honors freedom of choice, and is rooted in relationship. The former arrangement regarding the institution of leadership has reaped untold havoc in many congregations, while the latter is more apt to glean better results because it is informed not only by the Word of Christ but the Spirit of Christ. Inevitably, we will either embrace error and suffer the consequences, or we will endeavor to know the truth and enjoy the corresponding fruit of freedom.

## Identifying and Choosing Leaders

Now that we have a better understanding of what is meant by *obey* and *submit* in Hebrews 13:17 and we've seen that the church has *effectual* authority and responsibility to manage its own affairs, including the selection of leaders, *how* exactly is it supposed to identify and choose these leaders? Let's take a closer look at the qualifications for elders, deacons, or other leadership positions in the church and discover how leaders were appointed. What did the early church look for? What were some of the qualities the congregation sought to identify in the replacement for Judas in Acts 1 or those selected to serve the widows in Acts 6?

You may be surprised to discover that the Bible is much more concerned about leaders being *examples to imitate* instead of *rulers with authority* over others. See if you can discern this theme as we consider the following passages in Scripture. I will extract the key words and phrases from these passages that apply to leaders.

## 1 Peter 5:1–5

> So I exhort the elders among you, as a fellow elder and a witness of the sufferings of Christ, as well as a partaker in the glory that is going to be revealed: shepherd the flock of God that is among you, exercising oversight, not under compulsion, but willingly, as God would have you; not for shameful gain, but eagerly; not domineering over those in your charge, but being examples to the flock. And when the chief Shepherd appears, you will receive the unfading crown of glory. Likewise, you who are younger, be subject to the elders. Clothe yourselves, all of you, with humility toward one another,

for "God opposes the proud but gives grace to the humble."

Keywords/Phrases

- Shepherd
- Exercising oversight
- Not domineering over those in your charge
- Being examples to the flock
- Clothe yourselves, all of you, with humility toward one another
- God opposes the proud but gives grace to the humble

Some thoughts about *shepherding*: First, shepherds must be among the sheep. In order for an elder to shepherd the flock of God under his care, he must actually be *among* the people. In other words, he must be present, available, and accessible. However, I often hear laypeople complain about the *inaccessibility* of contemporary leadership: "It's hard to get a meeting with the elders. They seem so busy. They're always meeting, but not with us. You have to get an appointment well in advance. I see them on Sunday in the pulpit, but then I don't see them for the rest of the week. I think they have their own meetings." Second, what it means to *shepherd* is to extend care, protect, provide, guide, and be willing to lay down one's life for the sheep. Third, while he is shepherding, the shepherd doesn't micromanage the sheep. Instead, he exercises *oversight*—a word that connotes a broader, less intrusive kind of interaction.

## Philippians 3:17

> Brothers, join in imitating me, and keep your eyes on those who walk according to the example you have in us.

Keywords/Phrases

- Join in imitating me
- The example you have in us

Note that Paul does not *command* the elders to imitate him. Instead, he offers an encouraging invitation to *join* in imitating him. The fact that Paul does not presume an authority to rule over these elders is very instructive and is consistent with his leadership style throughout the whole of the New Testament. As shown by his word choice, Paul is more interested in demonstrating exemplary character for others to imitate than he is in exercising authority over them.

## 2 Thessalonians 3:7–9

> For you yourselves know how you ought to imitate us, because we were not idle when we were with you, nor did we eat anyone's bread without paying for it, but with toil and labor we worked night and day, that we might not be a burden to any of you. It was not because we do not have that right, but to give you in ourselves an example to imitate.

Keywords/Phrases

- You ought to imitate us
- To give you in ourselves an example to imitate

Again, we see an emphasis on leaders being worthy examples for others to imitate, staying humble and not haughty, proud, or condescending.

## 1 Timothy 4:11–16

> Command and teach these things. Let no one despise you for your youth, but set the believers an example in speech, in conduct, in love, in faith, in purity. Until I come, devote yourself to the public reading of Scripture, to exhortation, to teaching. Do not neglect the gift you have, which was given you by prophecy when the council of elders laid their hands on you. Practice these things, immerse yourself in them, so that all may see your progress. Keep a close watch on yourself and on the teaching. Persist in this, for by so doing you will save both yourself and your hearers.

Keywords/Phrases

- Command and teach these things

- Set the believers an example in speech, in conduct, in love, in faith, in purity
- Devote yourself to the public reading of Scripture, to exhortation, to teaching
- Practice these things, immerse yourself in them, so that all may see your progress
- Keep a close watch on yourself and on the teaching
- Persist in this, for by so doing you will save both yourself and your hearers

This passage is full of insights for those in leadership, mainly because it says that leaders should be less concerned with policing their congregants and more concerned with preaching, teaching, and being examples for their congregants to follow. I find it interesting that the Bible repeatedly instructs and encourages leaders to "keep a close watch," not on the members of their church but on *themselves* and on "the teaching," meaning Scripture. By doing this, the Bible says they will "save themselves and their hearers." In other words, the best way for a leader to promote biblical character qualities in the congregation is to exemplify those qualities in *himself*. There is nothing in the Bible about being a harsh taskmaster or "whipping the congregation into shape." Paul uses strong words like *practice* and *immerse* to emphasize the intensity with which leaders are to examine their own behavior so that the congregation may see their progress and provide an example for them to follow. In this way, it seems the spiritual health of a church is heavily influenced by the example of speech, conduct, love, faith, and purity of the leadership.

In order to properly understand the phrase "command and teach these things," we need to recognize that this exhortation still lies within the broader context and parameters of Scripture which prohibits leaders to command and teach their own opinions, agendas, or preferences. Leaders have complete liberty to strongly proclaim and declare, in the most robust manner, the teachings of *Scripture*—not their own extrabiblical material—and the congregation should enthusiastically encourage them to do so.

## Titus 2:7–8

> Show yourself in all respects to be a model of good works, and in your teaching show integrity, dignity, and sound speech that cannot be condemned, so that an opponent may be put to shame, having nothing evil to say about us.

Keywords/Phrases

- Show yourself
- A model of good works
- In your teaching show integrity, dignity, and sound speech
- That cannot be condemned
- An opponent may be put to shame
- Having nothing evil to say about us

Once again, we see an exhortation for leaders to pay close attention to themselves (not the congregation) and to be a model of good works for others to imitate and follow. Also, we see the positive impact of respectful, solid biblical teaching. Notice how Paul draws a connection between the character of the teacher and the integrity and soundness of the teaching, saying that opponents of the Gospel are silenced not by threats, intimidation, or ultimatums but by exemplary character and teaching. This is also what ultimately commends aspiring leaders to the congregation.

## Hebrews 13:7

> Remember your leaders, those who spoke to you the word of God. Consider the outcome of their way of life, and imitate their faith.

Keywords/Phrases

- Remember your leaders
- Who spoke to you the word of God
- Consider the outcome of their way of life
- Imitate their faith

As we consider the exhortation to "remember our leaders," it is important to understand that Scripture expects leaders to be of noble character and *worthy* to emulate, imitate, and follow. We are not called to remember or honor them because of their title or position but because of their exemplary way of life in both word and deed, "who spoke to you the Word of God." It is, therefore,

## Paul with Philemon: The Essence of Leadership

One of the most moving and compelling examples in the entire Bible that displays the proper function and disposition of a leader is found in the book of Philemon. In this book, Paul expresses his burden that Onesimus, an escaped slave, be restored to his master, Philemon, as a free man and brother in Christ.

Paul, at this time, is very likely at the end of his ministry, having been shipwrecked, hungry, stoned, left for dead, flogged, and eventually imprisoned. If any Christian has earned the right to command unquestioned obedience, it is the apostle Paul. However, Paul does not misuse or abuse his authority or his highly respected position to demand obedience. He doesn't give an ultimatum to Philemon. Instead, Paul *appeals* to Philemon with a disposition of profound humility and faith, exuding meekness and mutual respect toward Philemon as a brother in Christ and fellow believer. Rather than "pulling rank" and demanding obedience to his will, Paul assures Philemon he intends to do nothing without Philemon's consent (v. 14) because he considers Philemon a partner in the faith (v. 17). As such, Paul wants Philemon to *freely* respond to his request and not out of a sense of compulsion (v. 14).

It would be refreshing if more leaders today were to emulate this example instead of wielding an authority and power that Scripture does not condone or authorize! However, while it is incumbent on leaders to change their understanding and practice of leadership where necessary, it is more important for the *congregation* to recognize its duty to select humble candidates for leadership in the first place! Remember, it is only the collective members of a local church that have the effectual authority to actually authorize and implement changes in their congregation. While Scripture grants them declarative authority, leaders are not authorized to bring about whatever they determine or command for the congregation. This remains the privilege and responsibility of the Holy Spirit as manifested in the authority of the church. This truth is affirmed by such stalwarts of the faith as Louis Berkhof:

> The officers of the Church are the representatives of the people chosen by popular vote. This does not mean, however, that they receive their authority from the people, for the call of the people is but confirmation of the inner call by the Lord Himself; and it is from Him that they receive their authority and to Him that they are responsible. When they are called representatives, this is merely an indication of the fact that they were chosen to their office by the people, and does not imply that they derive their authority from them. At the same time, they are duty bound to recognize the power invested in the Church as a whole by seeking its assent or consent in important matters.[76]

---

[76] Louis Berkhof, *Systematic Theology* (Grand Rapids: Eerdmans, 1996), 584.

inferred that remembering our leaders is conditional upon their ability to meet these biblical prerequisites of good character and sound teaching. If leaders live unscrupulous lives and demonstrate poor faith, we are not called to follow them or to imitate their faith. This requirement of leaders being worthy of imitation and therefore commendable to follow and remember is also found in 1 Corinthians 4:16: "I urge you, then, be imitators of me," and 1 Corinthians 11:1: "Be imitators of me, as I am of Christ."

## Acts 20:28

> Pay careful attention to yourselves and to all the flock, in which the Holy Spirit has made you overseers, to care for the church of God, which he obtained with his own blood.

Keywords/Phrases

- Pay careful attention to yourselves and to all the flock
- The Holy Spirit has made you overseers
- To care for the church of God

It is a fair presumption (and good hermeneutics) to note that when the Bible wants to emphasize an important point, it repeats that point over and over again. We can see an example of this in the number of times and various ways Scripture has thus far emphasized how leaders are to pay careful attention to themselves first before they endeavor to pay careful attention to the flock of God, especially in a formal capacity as pastor, elder, or overseer.

# 1 Corinthians 4:1

This is how one should regard us, as servants of Christ and stewards of the mysteries of God.

Keywords/Phrases

- Servants of Christ
- Stewards of the mysteries of God

Now we come full circle to the original admonition and job description of leaders being *servants* of Christ, particularly in their relationship to God's people, and stewards of the "mysteries of God," which are the Scriptures. This expectation for leaders to be good stewards of the Word of God can also be seen in Paul's exhortation to Timothy: "Do your best to present yourself to God as one approved, a worker who has no need to be ashamed, rightly handling the word of truth" (2 Tim. 2:15).

Other biblical exhortations to leaders include the following:

- Leaders are to practice what they preach (Matt. 23:2–3).
- Leaders are not to "lord over" others (2 Cor. 1:23).
- Leadership is for the purpose of building up and not destroying (2 Cor. 10:8, 13:10).
- Leaders are to "command and teach" (1 Tim. 4:12).
- Leaders are not to be domineering over those in their charge (1 Peter 5:3).

# THE URIAH SYNDROME

And John Stott:

> The twelve [apostles] did not impose a solution on the church, however, but gathered all the disciples together in order to share the problem with them...In this incident, we discover the wisdom of strong pastoral leadership and appropriate congregational involvement. Even the apostles recognized that it was proper to involve the congregation in vital decision-making that would effect the life and ministry of the church.[77]

Unfortunately, this simple but profound doctrine of church authority has been widely disregarded throughout the evangelical church, as evidenced by the ever-increasing cry of spiritually abused saints in the body of Christ who continue to raise their voices against the misuse and abuse of authority in the church. Ultimately, the only way to still their voices and stop this abuse is if congregations accept their biblical responsibility and duty to bring about the changes they desire in their own churches. This is why I'm amazed that most evangelical churches seem to have their leaders chosen by *other leaders* with little to no consideration given to the desires of the congregation! What's worse, congregations don't even appear to have a *problem* with this arrangement—until, of course, they start to have concerns with the leadership. Even at this point, though, the congregation is typically helpless with no recourse provided

---

[77] John R. W. Stott, *The Message of Acts* (Downers Grove, IL: InterVarsity, 1990), 121.

in their bylaws, constitution, or book of church order. I often find that most congregants haven't even *read* these documents!

In the end, congregants discover their only real options are to complain among themselves or to make futile appeals to their leaders (who are not likely to concede authority, power, or position if they can help it). Typically, when a congregation is impotent and powerless to reform their church, unrest and division will soon follow. This is why the authority of the church should be taught and practiced as an integral component of church culture and memorialized in the constitution and by-laws of the local congregation.

As we have seen thus far, a congregation has the scriptural authority and responsibility to select its own leaders, who are to be evaluated on character, aptitude, and disposition. The task of choosing who would serve the widows in Acts 6 began with these instructions from the apostles: "Therefore, brothers, pick out from among you seven men of good repute, full of the Spirit and of wisdom, whom we will appoint to this duty" (Acts 6:3). The apostles did not presume to solve this problem by making executive decisions that excluded the participation of the congregation. Instead, they rightly delegated the responsibility to that local body of believers. They did this because they had been taught by Jesus to hold His body, the church, in high regard. Leaders throughout the early church understood and respected the authority and responsibility of the body of Christ and were convinced it had the spiritual gifting and aptitude necessary to accomplish whatever tasks it was called upon to perform. As we will see in the next chapter, the authority and competency of the church is illustrated throughout the New Testament.

# THE URIAH SYNDROME

I would like to conclude this chapter with another sobering exhortation on the duties and qualifications of leaders from Samuel Miller, who pastored for nearly half a century in New York City during the early 1800s. This excerpt is drawn from a sermon which was later expanded into a book on church leadership:

> We know that ministers are subject to the same frailties and imperfections with other men. We know, too, that a love of pre-eminence and of power is not only natural to them, in common with others; but that this principle, very early after the days of the Apostles, began to manifest itself as the reigning sin of ecclesiastics, and produced, first Prelacy, and afterwards Popery, which has so long and so ignobly enslaved the Church of Christ. Does not this plainly show the folly and danger of yielding undefined power to pastors alone? Is it wise or safe to constitute one man a despot over a whole Church? Is it proper to entrust to a single individual the weighty and complicated work of inspecting, trying, judging, admitting, condemning, excluding, and restoring, without control? Ought the members of a Church to consent that all their rights and privileges in reference to Christian communion, should be subject to the will of a single man, as his partiality, kindness, and favoritism, on the one hand; or his

caprice, prejudice, or passion, on the other, might dictate? Such a mode of conducting the government of the Church, to say nothing of its unscriptural character, is, in the highest degree, unreasonable and dangerous. It can hardly fail to exert an influence of the most injurious character, both on the clergy and laity. It tends to nurture in the former, a spirit of selfishness, pride and ambition; and instead of ministers of holiness, love, and mercy, to transform them into ecclesiastical tyrants. While its tendency, with regard to the latter, is gradually to beget in them a blind, implicit submission to clerical domination. The ecclesiastical encroachments and despotism of former times, already alluded to, read us a most instructive lesson on this subject. The fact is, committing the whole government of the Church to the hands of pastors alone, may be affirmed to carry in it some of the worst seeds of Popery, which, though under the administration of good men, they may not at once lead to palpable mischief, will seldom fail in producing, in the end, the most serious evils, both to those who govern, and those who obey.[78]

---

[78] Samuel Miller, *An Essay on the Warrant, Nature, and Duties of the Office of the Ruling Elder* (Philadelphia: Presbyterian Board of Education, 1832), 180–181.

It would be unbalanced and overly pessimistic not to commend and acknowledge leaders throughout the body of Christ who *do* remain tireless servants of those to whom they extend care and who consider it anathema to misuse or abuse their privilege to shepherd the flock of God under their care. I'm thankful that a healthy contingent of diligent and faithful leaders still seeks to follow the Lord's admonition to be the servant of all. As all leaders embrace their gift and calling to care for God's people and preach His Word, may it not be at the expense of those they are charged to serve. I pray that they instead demonstrate the grace and humility of Christ so they, together with their congregations, would experience "times of refreshment" (Acts 3:20) and the wonderful benefits and blessings of the Lord.

# Study Notes

# 10

# THE AUTHORITY OF THE CHURCH

*If he refuses to listen to them, tell it to the church. And if he refuses to listen even to the church, let him be to you as a Gentile and a tax collector. Truly, I say to you, whatever you bind on earth shall be bound in heaven, and whatever you loose on earth shall be loosed in heaven.*

—Matthew 18:17–18

*Church authority, grounded in the Word of Christ, is also limited to it. Christian obedience to church rule is obedience in the Lord, for His Word governs the church.*

—Edmund Clowney, *The Church*

Have you ever noticed that the vast majority of the letters in the New Testament are addressed "to the saints"? These letters are addressed to *whole churches* (or groups of churches) and not just to the church leaders!⁷⁹ Compare that to today's church culture, in which leaders are too often considered the only ones biblically responsible to ensure the integrity and fidelity of preaching of God's Word. This, as we've seen, is not the view of the Bible.

Yes, those who preach and teach should be diligent as they endeavor to feed the sheep, but as renowned theologian Robert Saucy reminds us, "The responsibility of maintaining true doctrine and practice is directed toward the entire church."⁸⁰ It is the *congregation's* duty to protect itself from error, false teaching, and heresy. Those who sit in the pews must be just as diligent in studying Scripture as those who stand in the pulpit, as Daniel Akin recognizes:

> [T]he calling to pursue doctrinal fidelity is ultimately held in trust, under God, by the congregation.... It is crucial to see that whenever the authors of scripture combat false teaching, *they write to the churches, because doctrinal integrity is a matter of congregational responsibility* [emphasis mine].⁸¹

Such an awesome responsibility should encourage every parishioner to be like the Bereans who examined the Word daily

---

[79] Nineteen of the twenty-one letters are written to individual churches or groups of churches; and the other two, Philemon and 3 John, are addressed to two individuals: Philemon and John's friend Gaius. Neither individual is addressed as a leader.

[80] Robert L. Saucy, *The Church in God's Program* (Chicago: Moody, 1972), 116.

[81] Daniel Akin, "The Single-Elder-Led Church," in *Perspectives on Church Government: Five Views of Church Polity*, edited by Chad Owen Brand and R. Stanton Norman (Nashville: B&H, 2004), 34.

and received it with eagerness! I urge you to consider the implication of these truths, for we've already seen that God Himself places His utmost confidence in the spiritual aptitude of the local church to capably manage its own affairs. It is no mere coincidence that the majority of New Testament letters are specifically addressed to churches, not leaders. Rather, it intentionally shows how highly the authors of Scripture esteemed and respected the churches they served and reflects the serious tasks and responsibilities the church was engaged in throughout the New Testament.

Indeed, the Scriptures show congregations as being eager to understand and embrace their responsibilities and calling as the body of Christ, with leaders who hold them in high esteem and who have great confidence in their ability to accomplish all that God expects. These leaders understood the church to be a unique manifestation of the presence of Christ Himself and therefore able to discern the wisdom and will of God as its people prayed and worshipped together in unity—for Jesus promised He would be wherever two or three were gathered in His name (Matt. 18:20).

In this chapter, I want to challenge errant views of church authority and instead cultivate in you a biblical understanding, along with its application for the congregation. Some may find the notion of the church having *any* authority a surprising proposition, but we will see from Scripture it was quite common for even fledgling congregations in the New Testament to exercise authority as their members enthusiastically carried out the daily affairs of church life. We will also look at how the authority of the church was considered to be orthodox theology by many scholars throughout church history.

We saw in the previous chapter that Jesus, in Matthew 20:25–28, taught that His church would not be characterized by the same top-down authority structure found in the secular world of his day. As professor Gerald Cowen reminds us,

> There is no hierarchy in the body of Christ. All the members have equal value before God. They must work together to make the body function in a manner that glorifies God. As it has been pointed out, all believers have spiritual gifts that are necessary for the body to function completely. All believers are priests who have full access to God Himself.[82]

What then should church leadership, submission, and governance look like? To start, let's look at Matthew 16:13–19, one of the first places in the New Testament where church authority is addressed and where the authority of the church is rooted:

> Now when Jesus came into the district of Caesarea Philippi, he asked his disciples, "Who do people say that the Son of Man is?" And they said, "Some say John the Baptist, others say Elijah, and others Jeremiah or one of the prophets." He said to them, "But who do you say that I am?" Simon Peter replied, "You are the Christ, the Son of the living God." And Jesus answered him, "Blessed are you, Simon Bar-Jonah! For flesh and blood

---

[82] Gerald P. Cowen, *Who Rules the Church?* (Nashville: B&H, 2003), 96.

has not revealed this to you, but my Father who is in heaven. And I tell you, you are Peter, and on this rock I will build my church, and the gates of hell shall not prevail against it. I will give you the keys of the kingdom of heaven, and whatever you bind on earth shall be bound in heaven, and whatever you loose on earth shall be loosed in heaven."

This passage is crucial to understand, and Jonathan Leeman's interpretation of it is so good that I want to include it here at length:

> It's worth noticing the parallel grammar between Peter's "You are the Christ" and Jesus' "You are Peter." Peter had just defined Jesus' identity and role in redemptive history—He is the Messiah, the Son of the living God. Jesus defines Peter's identity and role in redemptive history—he is the rock or foundation on which the church will be built. Hence there is a play on words between *petros* (Peter) and *petra* (*rock*). This church will be the true church, not some false church hell can prevail against....Theologian Edmund Clowney puts it this way: "The confession cannot be separated from Peter, neither can Peter be separated from his confession."... We discover that Christ begins building His church on the *rightly confessing Peter*, not just on

Peter and Peter's confession. The ambassador doesn't travel without the king's edict, and the edict doesn't travel without the king's ambassador....How does Jesus then build upon this confessing Peter, or, rather, what does Peter *do* in his capacity of the foundation? We find that Jesus answers that question in the next verse: "I will give you the keys of the kingdom of heaven, and whatever you bind on earth shall be bound in heaven, and whatever you loose on earth shall be loosed in heaven" (v. 19)....[E]veryone seems to agree that He is giving Peter authority by giving him the keys of the kingdom. Further, I think we can say, somewhat uncontroversially, that the connection between verses 18 and 19 means that "the church is the agency of kingdom authority on earth."...Perhaps more controversially, I would argue that the kingdom will be extended through the church *alone*, since no other organization or individual on earth has been given the keys of the kingdom— not philanthropic organizations, social agencies, governments, political parties, or even well-meaning individuals....In Matthew 18 the same phrase concerning binding and loosing is again used, only this time the keys of the kingdom are not explicitly mentioned, and the "you" is plural: "Truly, I say to you, whatever you bind on earth shall be bound in heaven, and whatever you loose on earth shall be loosed in heaven" (v. 18).[83]

To summarize, we see the origin of church authority in Matthew 16 where Jesus affirms the *rightly confessing Peter* ("You are the Christ, the Son of the living God"), which is the bedrock confession that marks an authentic church, and we see the *application* of that authority in Matthew 18. We also learn from Matthew 18 that the local church is instructed to be the final authority and arbitrator in matters of discipline within the congregation of believers. Such authority is exclusive to the church and not meant to be given to a single individual or group of spiritual elites. Furthermore, we know that Jesus did not intend for Peter to function as a pope since Jesus prohibits hierarchical forms of government in Matthew 20:25–28.

Without question, Jesus's prohibition of a hierarchical authority structure, in conjunction with His giving the power and authority to "bind" and "loose" points to the church as being the only authorized entity permitted to exercise effectual authority for the congregation. Effectual authority, once again, is the power to *make effectual* that which is declared, like excommunicating or restoring believers to membership in the church. Like Leeman says, the church is the "agency of kingdom authority on earth." We can see this illustrated in Jesus's instruction on church discipline:

> If your brother sins against you, go and tell him his fault, between you and him alone.

---

[83] Jonathan Leeman, *The Surprising Offense of God's Love* (Wheaton, IL: Crossway. 2010), 178–180.

> If he listens to you, you have gained your brother. But if he does not listen, take one or two others along with you, that every charge may be established by the evidence of two or three witnesses. If he refuses to listen to them, tell it to the church. And if he refuses to listen even to the church, let him be to you as a Gentile and a tax collector. Truly, I say to you, whatever you bind on earth shall be bound in heaven, and whatever you loose on earth shall be loosed in heaven. Again I say to you, if two of you agree on earth about anything they ask, it will be done for them by my Father in heaven. For where two or three are gathered in my name, there am I among them. (Matt. 18:15–20)

Did you notice that this passage has, conspicuously, no reference to deacons, elders, bishops, or leaders of any kind? This is intentional. By leaving out any mention of leadership, the text clearly presumes the congregation's calling, gifting, and responsibility to mediate its own affairs and stand as the final authority when it comes to "binding" and "loosing" people in church discipline and restoration. Such authority is sobering and profound and has wisely been given by Christ to the church itself rather than to any other individuals or groups. As we saw in the previous chapter, while leaders have the *declarative* authority to teach and preach the holy Word of God, under no circumstance do they possess the *effectual* authority to enact changes in the congregation. This authority is exclusively ascribed *to* the congregation. When leaders insist on possessing and exercising effectual authority over the congregation, they are actually usurping the authority of Christ Himself since His authority is supernaturally manifested by His Spirit in the church. This grave and frightful error is akin to Satan's desire to be greater than or equal to God in the book of Isaiah:

> "You said in your heart,
> 'I will ascend to heaven;
> above the stars of God
> I will set my throne on high;
> I will sit on the mount of assembly
> in the far reaches of the north;
> I will ascend above the heights of the clouds;
> I will make myself like the Most High.'" (Isa. 14:13–14)

It is no wonder that Paul and the other New Testament leaders held each local church in such high esteem, even when they were in need of correction like the Corinthians or the Galatians. Unlike many in leadership today, we see the apostles and elders in Scripture seeking the participation and advice of these churches, calling upon them to make important decisions. Professor Robert Wring gives some historical perspective:

> The congregational model was widely practiced in the first century New Testament church, apparently by theological design. This was the only form of government practiced among primitive Christians until the second century when changes began to be made in church

polity. The elder and deacons could make their voice heard in any matter pertaining to the church's welfare, but they did not have exclusive governmental prerogative. Under Christ, the whole congregation was the final court of appeal.

In the Book of Acts, many important decisions were made by individual congregations. It was the entire church that chose the first deacons in Acts 6:5. In Acts 13:1–4, the whole church sent out Barnabas and Saul to do mission work, and in Acts 15, the Jerusalem Council included the messengers from at least one local congregation from Antioch (verse 23), as well as the believers in the Jerusalem assembly. Paul instructed the Corinthian church to be responsible believers and take charge of their own affairs. The local congregation at Corinth was admonished to correct the problem of internal strife among its fellowship, to do what was necessary to ensure the proper observance of the Lord's Supper, and to take action in exercising discipline in order to preserve the purity of its church membership (1 Corinthians 1:10; 11:33–34; and 5:3–5, 12–13). Neither the elders nor the deacons interfered with the exercise of a congregational church government.[84]

## How to Appoint Elders

Throughout Scripture, we see elders and deacons being appointed—first by the apostles, then later by other elders. This is confirmed throughout church history as the normal and orthodox means by which leadership roles were recognized and established *in* the church. But what did that process look like? Did an apostle or elder show up at a specific church and simply choose one of its members to be the leader, or was the church itself involved in this process?

A plain reading of Scripture shows that the task of appointing new leadership was a complimentary process in which a congregation worked *together* with current leaders. The congregation *chose* prospective leaders from among their own number; then the apostles or elders *appointed* those selected individuals publicly by laying hands on them together with the congregation and committing them to the Lord. Let's first look at Acts 1:15 and 1:21–26, where the church was involved in choosing a replacement for Judas:

> Peter stood up among the brothers (the company of persons was in all about 120) and said…"[O]ne of the men who have accompanied us during all the time that the Lord Jesus went in and out among us, beginning

---

[84] Robert A. Wring, "Elder Rule and Southern Baptist Church Polity," *Journal for Baptist Theology and Ministry* 3, no. 1 (Spring 2005): 191–192.

> from the baptism of John until the day when he was taken up from us—one of these men must become with us a witness to his resurrection." And they put forward two, Joseph called Barsabbas, who was also called Justus, and Matthias. And they prayed and said, "You, Lord, who know the hearts of all, show which one of these two you have chosen to take the place in this ministry and apostleship from which Judas turned aside to go to his own place." And they cast lots for them, and the lot fell on Matthias, and he was numbered with the eleven apostles.

In this passage, Peter (a leader) appeals to the 120 believers (the congregation) that a replacement for Judas (a leader) is necessary. Those 120 believers (the congregation) select two candidates from among their own number to be considered for the new leadership position. The joint action of Peter (a leader) and the 120 (the church) results in the successful appointment of Matthias as a new leader.

Next, let's look at Acts 6:2–6:

> And the twelve summoned the full number of the disciples [meaning: the congregation] and said, "It is not right that we should give up preaching the word of God to serve tables. Therefore, brothers, pick out from among you seven men of good repute, full of the Spirit and of wisdom, whom we will

> appoint to this duty. But we will devote ourselves to prayer and to the ministry of the word." And what they said pleased the whole gathering, and they chose Stephen, a man full of faith and of the Holy Spirit, and Philip, and Prochorus, and Nicanor, and Timon, and Parmenas, and Nicolaus, a proselyte of Antioch. These they set before the apostles, and they prayed and laid their hands on them.

We see the same principle as before: the congregation of believers selected candidates for leadership from among their own number, who were then ratified—"appointed"—by the incumbent leaders. Thus, we can see the distinction between "selecting" and "appointing" that occurs numerous times in the New Testament. F. F. Bruce explains, "It was the community as a whole that *selected* these seven men and presented them to the apostles for their approbation; it was the apostles that *appointed* them to their office [emphasis mine]."[85]

We can confidently assume the same process occurred in every church since Paul and Barnabas appointed elders in the churches they visited (Acts 14:23), and Paul's instruction to Titus was likewise to "appoint elders in every town" (Titus 1:5). Since the examples we just saw in Acts 1 and 6 were at the very *beginning* of the early church, it is highly unlikely that Paul, Barnabas, Titus, or any other leader would later enter a town, gather the local church, then select elders for that church without the participation of the rest of the congregation. This would not be consistent with the teaching and examples we

---

[85] F. F. Bruce, *The Book of Acts* (Grand Rapids: Eerdmans, 1988), 122.

just reviewed, nor would it have been wise for them to assume they had better insight and discernment than the congregation in knowing which prospective leaders best met the criteria of 1 Timothy 3:1–13. After all, church members likely knew the candidates well and were in a far better position to ensure the prospective leaders met the biblical criteria than Paul or any of the other apostles who would appoint the new leaders. This is one of the reasons why the apostle Paul expends great effort persuading his readers and hearers to embrace the wonderful truth that *every Christian* is uniquely gifted and *necessary* for the whole body to function as it was designed, as he says here:

> To each is given the manifestation of the Spirit for the common good. For to one is given through the Spirit the utterance of wisdom, and to another the utterance of knowledge according to the same Spirit, to another faith by the same Spirit, to another gifts of healing by the one Spirit, to another the working of miracles, to another prophecy, to another the ability to distinguish between spirits, to another various kinds of tongues, to another the interpretation of tongues. All these are empowered by one and the same Spirit, *who apportions to each one individually as he wills* [emphasis mine]. (1 Cor. 7:11)

And here:

> God arranged the members in the body, each one of them, as he chose. If all were a single member, where would the body be? As it is, there are many parts, yet one body. The eye cannot say to the hand, "I have no need of you," nor again the head to the feet, "I have no need of you. (1 Cor. 12:18–21)

This is exactly why God gives the responsibility for making weighty decisions and judgments (like the task of excommunicating or restoring other believers) exclusively to the congregation as a whole (Matt. 18:17) and not to the sole discretion of any individual—regardless of how learned and gifted he may be. Otherwise, every believer would be subject to the limited discretion and discernment of an isolated individual or group instead of the whole *church*, which is *the fullness of Christ* Himself (Eph. 1:23). As the embodiment of Christ, something mysteriously wonderful and powerful happens when the church assembles. When the gathered people of God meet and seek Him together in prayer, worship, and unity, they can anticipate being of one mind, miraculously embody all the gifts of His Spirit, and are able to ascertain God's wisdom and will with regard to all important church matters. While individual believers certainly enjoy all the benefits of Christ's redemptive work and corresponding blessings, there is a certain manifestation of Christ and His fullness that is particular, unique, and exclusive to a gathered church. This is why the apostles and other leaders of the New Testament had no hesitation including the church in important matters like

- choosing leaders (Acts 1:22; 6:3),
- affirming the content of important correspondence and doctrine sent to other churches (Acts 15:22–35),
- deciding who would be sent in the name of the church (Acts 11:22; 13:1–3; 15:3; 17:10, 14),
- deciding who would carry offerings in the name of the church (Acts 11:29–30; 1 Corinthians 16:3–4),
- making godly judgments amongst themselves (1 Cor. 6:1–5),
- exercising church discipline (Matt. 18:15–20),
- restoring a repentant believer to the congregation (2 Cor. 2:6–8).

This means that no single leader, scholar, or any other individual possesses all the gifts of the Spirit—something explicitly clear from Scripture:

> To each is given the manifestation of the Spirit for the common good. (1 Cor. 12:11)
>
> All these are empowered by one and the same Spirit, who apportions to each one individually as he wills. (1 Cor. 12:7)
>
> The eye cannot say to the hand, "I have no need of you," nor again the head to the feet, "I have no need of you." (1 Cor. 12:21)

God, in His great wisdom, made us interdependent so that we, through mutually expressed love and humility, might acknowledge the need for one another's gifts and, thereby, enjoy the amazing wonder of *all* the gifts of the Spirit and the *fullness* of Christ by coming together as His body. In addition, the gathering of the church enjoys the presence of Christ and, therefore, has the capacity to manifest His discernment, mercy, wisdom, and knowledge—to the extent that the decisions made by the church should be respected as *the will of Christ Himself.*

Manifesting the presence of Christ in the church is also crucial for evangelism. The entire world aches for a true manifestation of the living God, and a fractured, divided church cannot manifest the presence of Christ, for He is not divided (1 Cor. 1:13). This means that leaders and congregants who refuse to recognize the authority of the church are actually preventing the church from fulfilling one of its fundamental missions—to be the testimony of God to a needy world. This is why Jesus prays so earnestly for His people to be unified as He and the Father are unified—"[I ask] for those who will believe in me through their word, *that they may all be one*, just as you, Father, are in me, and I in you, that they also may be in us, *so that the world may believe that you have sent me* [emphases mine]" (John 17:20–21).

This amazing truth should motivate us to gather together as a chosen race, a royal priesthood, a holy nation, and a people for his own possession, that we may proclaim the excellencies of Him who called us out of darkness into His marvelous light (1 Peter 2:9)! Only as the individual members of the body "become one" can they enjoy such a comprehensive manifestation of Christ. No single individual has the capacity to function in the same measure, gifting, and fullness, which is exactly why leaders should defer to the body of Christ on important church matters. The *mind* of Christ is made manifest in the *body* of Christ. God, in his wisdom, has designed the church to function this way.

This is also why the apostles in Acts 1 gathered the 120 believers to begin the process of finding a replacement instead of cloistering themselves from the rest of the church. Similarly, in Acts 6, we saw the apostles avail themselves of the collective wisdom, discernment, and authority of the church to determine who would serve the widows so that the apostles themselves could preach the Word. In response, *the congregation chose* seven men they deemed worthy for the role. This is perhaps the first evidence of how the church went about selecting deacons. Charles Spurgeon likewise recognized this process of selection as normative practice for the church:

> To our minds, the Scripture seems very explicit as to how this Church should be ordered. We believe that every Church member should have equal rights and privileges; that *there is no power in Church officers to execute anything unless they have the full authorization of the members of the Church* [emphasis mine]. We believe, however, that the Church should choose its pastor, and having chosen him, that they should love him and respect him for his work's sake; that with him should be associated the deacons of the Church to take the oversight of pecuniary matters; and

> the elders of the Church to assist in all the works of the pastorate in the fear of God, being overseers of the flock. Such a Church we believe to be scripturally ordered; and if it abide in the faith, rooted, and grounded, and settled, such a Church may expect the benediction of heaven, and so it shall become the pillar and ground of the truth.[86]

Still, wouldn't it have been more efficient for the apostles to simply hold a private meeting isolated from the rest of the church, where they could decide themselves who would replace Judas and which individuals would serve the widows? After all, these men personally spent three years with Jesus. They listened to all His teachings and witnessed all His miracles. If there was ever a group of individuals qualified to make important and authoritative decisions for the church, it was these men! Yet they still took time to gather the church together in order to address these problems. They understood that *even they*, the twelve apostles, neither constituted the fullness of Christ the way the church does when its members are gathered together, nor would have manifested all the gifts of the many-membered body. They had to avail themselves of meeting together *with* the whole congregation of believers to experience those realities. To reiterate, the original apostles, discipled and taught by the Lord Himself, who knew Jesus in a very unique way—unlike anyone else who has lived since that time—*still refused* to make important decisions for the church without the participation of

---

[86] Charles Spurgeon, *The Metropolitan Tabernacle Pulpit*, vol. 7 (Pasadena, TX: Pilgrim Press, 1969), 658–659.

the body of Christ! Today, however, many leaders seem to practice the very opposite. They separate themselves from the rest of the congregation and cut themselves off from the very gifts they likely are lacking—all in order to make unilateral decisions affecting the entire church. This is a travesty.

Another example in which the congregation played an integral role was during the theological discussions and concluding decision of the Jerusalem Council in Acts 15. This was a watershed meeting that was held to determine whether or not Gentile Christians had to observe the Mosaic law. The church was present for the entire discussion and listened carefully as Peter, James, and others presented arguments. As the passage below indicates, the church participated together with all the elders and apostles in order to come to a consensus and give its approval on one of the most important doctrinal decisions in the New Testament. The congregation then selected emissaries to spread word of the council's decision to other churches:

> Then it seemed good to the apostles and the elders, *with the whole church* [emphasis mine], to choose men from among them and send them to Antioch with Paul and Barnabas. *They* (the whole congregation of believers) sent Judas called Barsabbas, and Silas, leading men among the brothers. (Acts 15:22)

These are only a few examples that demonstrate the high regard of the church held by the New Testament leaders as well as the confidence those leaders placed in the church's ability to participate in and resolve important matters in the daily life of the congregation. The Bible repeatedly shows that the apostles held the church in very high esteem, knowing the congregation would shoulder awesome responsibilities in the days to come.

But what about today's leaders? Are they just as eager to avail themselves of the collective gifts and callings inherent in the body of Christ? Or do they rather prefer expedience and control, making executive decisions without the congregation's input or approval? I expect that you see a stark difference, for leaders in the New Testament did not separate themselves from their fellow brothers and sisters in Christ. Rather, they gathered *together* with them and involved the entire congregation in making vital decisions and praying through difficult issues. In so doing, these leaders availed themselves of the fullness of Christ, replete with all the gifts of His Spirit. In these cases, the church was connected and unified with each member respecting one another's unique role and *depending* upon one another to ascertain and execute the will of God. This process of working together with churches was *normative* for the apostles, who knew it was necessary in order for healthy congregations to thrive. This is why they addressed their letters to the churches.

Again—is this the attitude and perspective of today's leaders and laypeople toward the church? Could it be that most of the turmoil, scandal, division, unrest, and abuse we regularly hear so much about today is the result of ignoring this powerful truth?

I think it is.

Otherwise, why would Christians, whom God *designed* to shine forth in a dark world as a witness of His own presence and power, continue to allow themselves to be marginalized and suppressed? Too many Christians today seem to *expect* this kind of marginalization to be business as usual. They appear to lack any confidence in knowing who they are as the body of Christ. Clearly, Paul's exhortation to Timothy is as relevant today as when he first wrote it

> I am writing these things to you so that, if I delay, you may know how one ought to behave in the household of God, *which is the church of the living God, a pillar and buttress of the truth* [emphasis mine]. (1 Timothy 3:14–16)

## The Institutionalization of the Church

What's behind all this? Where have we gone wrong? Why is the modern church succumbing to apathy and trading its authority, responsibility, and the very presence of Christ for an anemic, rank-and-file system that functions more like a business than the pillar and foundation of truth for whom Christ endured the cross? Professor and pastor Alexander Strauch offers this explanation:

> Some of the worst havoc wrought to the Christian faith has been a direct result of unscriptural forms of church structure. Only a few centuries after the apostles' death, for example, Christian churches began to assimilate both Roman and Jewish concepts of status, power, and priesthood. As a result, church government was clericalized and sacralized. Under Christ's name an elabo-

rately structured institution emerged that corrupted the simple, family structure of the apostolic churches, robbed God's people of their lofty position and ministry in Christ, and exchanged Christ's supremacy over His people for the supremacy of the institutional church.[87]

Based on your own personal study of the Scriptures, do you believe Jesus intended for a single individual (a priest, bishop, elder, modern apostle, etc.) or group of individuals (pastors, elders, a denominational committee, a convention, a synod, etc.) to exercise unilateral authority over others and even the entire congregation? Or do you believe there is "one mediator between God and men, the man Christ Jesus" (1 Timothy 2:5), not just in the context of salvation but also in the context of sanctification?

Do you believe Christ has equipped you, by His Spirit, with the ability to hear His voice, discern His will, and receive guidance, wisdom, and insight as you pray, study the Bible, and hear His Word taught and preached? Or do you believe that God has authorized someone else to do these things on your behalf in order to inform you of God's will for your life?

Your answers to all these questions will have profound repercussions for your personal life as well as for your spouse, your family, and your church. They also will determine what you perceive your responsibilities to be as a vital member in the body of Christ.

---

[87] Alexander Strauch, *Biblical Eldership* (Colorado Springs: Lewis & Roth, 2003), 101.

Theologian Wayne Grudem warns us not to ascribe undue spiritual superiority or power to an individual who uses a title of leadership to connote a possession of greater authority, anointing, or importance than any other layperson in the church. Though he specifically addresses the term *apostle* as problematic, his warning is relevant regardless of what title a leader may use, particularly if the intent is to distinguish oneself from the rest of the church as possessing greater spiritual authority or superiority.

> Though some may use the word *apostle* in English today to refer to very effective church planters or evangelists, it seems inappropriate and unhelpful to do so, for it simply confuses people who read the New Testament and see the high authority that is attributed to the office of "apostle" there. It is noteworthy that no major leader in the history of the church—not Athanasius or Augustine, not Luther or Calvin, not Wesley or Whitefield—has taken to himself the title of "apostle" or let himself be called an apostle. If any in modern times want to take the title "apostle" to themselves, they immediately raise the suspicion that they may be motivated by inappropriate pride and desires for self-exaltation, along with excessive ambition and a desire for more authority in the church than any one person should rightfully have.[88]

---

[88] Wayne Grudem, *Systematic Theology* (Grand Rapids: Zondervan, 1994), 911.

## The Priesthood of All Believers

If, in response to the questions above, you answered that you believe Christ has equipped you, by His Spirit, with the ability to hear His voice, discern His will, and receive spiritual wisdom, then you believe in a doctrine called the *priesthood of all believers*, sometimes called the doctrine of *universal priesthood*. Along with the authority of the church, the failure to understand this doctrine has riddled the church with all manner of dysfunction, disgrace, and scandal. Because the spiritual health of a congregation is usually an extension of the spiritual vibrancy of the individual members, these two doctrines exist in a sort of symbiotic relationship, where neglecting one causes the *other* to likewise be compromised. This creates a downward spiral that harms the congregation as well as the leaders.

For example, compromising or ignoring the priesthood of all believers causes a Christian to lose confidence in the ability to hear God's voice, determine His will, and ascertain God's direction for one's life. This will have a negative effect on one's confidence and conviction to embrace their responsibility as a functioning member in the congregation. Similarly, refusing to acknowledge the authority of the church will inevitably foster a low and anemic view of one's personal spiritual ability to *be* an active, vital member in the body of Christ. Therefore, it behooves every believer to study these two important doctrines with the enthusiasm of the Bereans, "examining the Scriptures daily to see if these things were so" (Acts 17:10–11).

Prior to studying the doctrine of the priesthood of all believers, I used to refer to it as the priesthood of the *believer* (singular). However, the Bible always refers to priesthood as a plural noun, so the term is not meant to signify a unique ministry or function that a believer possesses apart from the congregation of other saints.

This doctrine explains that when an individual becomes a born-again Christian, he also, by virtue of his new life in Christ, simultaneously becomes a priest of God and enters into the kingdom and royal priesthood of believers which, by definition, comprises the church. God spoke about the future coming of this priesthood in the Old Testament when he said to His people, "You shall be [future tense] to me a kingdom of priests and a holy nation" (Exo. 19:5–6), and "You shall be called [future tense] priests of the Lord; they shall speak [future tense] of the ministers of our God" (Isa. 61:6).

The New Testament, however, talks about this priesthood as something that has already been installed. John, in his vision, said, "To him who loves us and has freed us from our sins by his blood and made [past tense] us a kingdom, priests to his God and Father, to him be glory and dominion forever and ever" (Rev. 1:5–6). Later, John says the angels themselves say, "You have made [past tense] them a kingdom and priests to our God, and they shall reign on the earth" (Rev. 5:10). Peter wrote to a whole group of churches and said, "But you are [present tense] a chosen race, a royal priesthood, a holy nation, a people for his own possession, that you may proclaim the excellencies of him who called you out of darkness into his marvelous light" (1 Peter 2:9).

This means the promise of the Old Testament has since become a reality! Through the redeeming work of Christ, we have not only escaped the wrath of God but also have been ushered into a kingdom of priests where we can come directly before God Himself without the aid or mediation of a religious stand-in. Is this not amazing? We *ourselves* can enter the holy of holies. We *ourselves* can approach the throne of grace as needed. These truths should give us great confidence that God has indeed equipped us to perform the ministry He has given us as His people—and this ministry includes being essential to the most weighty and critical matters pertaining to one's local congregation. Our confidence as believers is predicated on the sacrificial work of Christ so that we might become a royal priesthood commissioned to take the message of the Gospel to a needy world and to exemplify Christ in the church where we serve.

This responsibility and authority of ministering in the royal priesthood granted to us *by* Christ is only legitimate and effectual in the context of being linked *to* the body of Christ. No individual is authorized to function as a priest over and above the congregation of other believers (who are priests themselves), but all believers share a common dignity and function within the context of the body of Christ. In fact, as Cyril Eastwood notes,

> The word "priest" and "priesthood" are never applied in the New Testament to the office of the Ministry. Even in the extensive list of Church officers and activities in 1 Corinthians 12:28–30 and Ephesians 4:11–12 there is no mention of priests. In fact, there are but two forms of priesthood in the New Testament— the Priesthood of Christ (Hebrews 6:20 and

7:26–8:7) and the Priesthood of all Believers (1 Peter 2:9 and Revelation 5:10).[89]

Unfortunately, by the late 1500s, the idea of a royal *kingdom* of priests had evolved into a royal *class* of priests:

> All authority was given unto the Bishop who unquestionably controlled the Church's teaching, worship, discipline, and ministry, and in an ill-defined and mystical sense he controlled also that most sacred treasure of Gospel—the offer of divine grace. This sort of teaching persisted in the Church without any serious or decisive opposition until the appearance of Martin Luther in the sixteenth century.[90]

Luther is famous in church history for spearheading the Reformation, a watershed movement in which the church began to regain important spiritual ground it had lost in the previous centuries. Luther fought well to reestablish many precious biblical truths, like the priesthood of all believers, whose neglect had produced an anemic and impotent church vulnerable to a host of dangerous heresies:

> Therefore everyone who knows that he is a Christian should be fully assured that all of

---

[89] Cyril Eastwood, *The Priesthood of All Believers* (Eugene, OR: Wipf and Stock, 1962), x.
[90] Ibid., xii

> us alike are priests, and that we all have the same authority in regard to the Word and the Sacraments, although no one has the right to administer them without the consent of the members of his Church, and the call of the majority.[91]

Like Luther stated, *all* believers possess, by virtue of their new birth in Christ, the ability to hear God's voice (John 10:27) and receive His wisdom (James 3:15), counsel (Isaiah 9:6), and direction (Proverbs 3:6). They must never allow their conscience to be violated or usurped by others (2 Corinthians 1:24) but must be persuaded by His Word and Spirit, to test everything and hold fast to what is good (1 Thessalonians 5:21). God shows no partiality (Romans 2:11) and has adequately equipped every believer with every good work (2 Timothy 3:17) as an integral part of our new life in Christ—without regard to education, status, or title.

Our faith in these truths is one of the most important means by which God protects us from falling prey to spiritual abuse, false teachers, and being led astray by deceptive doctrines. For instance, it is imperative that no Christian, regardless of the pressure and insistence from other believers, allows his conscience or personal convictions to be violated against their will, but this is precisely what authoritarian leaders attempt to do! Of course, it benefits every believer to submit to sound teaching, counsel, and wisdom which is informed by the Word of God—but *never* out of carnal fear, manipulation, threats, or

---

[91] Bertram Lee Woolf, *Reformation Writings of Martin Luther*, vol. 1 (London: Lutterworth Press, 1952), 318.

coercion (Prov. 11:14; 24:6). Martin Luther, facing imminent death for a heresy charge, famously stood by this principle. He struck a chord in 1521 that still resonates today when he said,

> Unless I am convinced by the testimony of the Scriptures or by clear reason (for I do not trust either in the pope or in councils alone, since it is well known that they have often erred and contradicted themselves), I am bound by the Scriptures I have quoted and my conscience is captive to the Word of God. I cannot and will not recant anything, since it is neither safe nor right to go against conscience. May God help me. Amen.[92]

Luther personified the concept of the priesthood of believers, and most of his writings and actions helped spark the Reformation. We and our congregations today ought to give renewed consideration to believing and practicing this important doctrine in the hope of experiencing our own reformation. In the excerpt below, Professor Wring emphasizes the critical importance of the priesthood of all believers and the dangers of compromising or nullifying this doctrine. Notice how he draws the connection between the priesthood of the individual believer and the authority of the church.

> Authority within the local church rests with the individual members of the congrega-

---

[92] Martin Brecht, *Martin Luther: His Road to Reformation, 1483–1521* (Minneapolis: Fortress, 1985), 460.

tion as they meet corporately. No matter what kind of polity Southern Baptist leaders choose to use, no one has the right to exercise any other kind of authority independently of, or contrary to, the wishes of the people who have chosen them as their leaders. The priesthood of the believer makes the entire church the proper decision-making body capable of making decisions that affect their community lives....[T]he final authority in the church resides in the corporate membership. The principle of democratic congregationalism works well in the local church because it is the natural outworking of the priesthood of all believers within the parameters of the local church.

The pastor, deacons, and other leaders work together as a team in helping the congregation in seeking the will of Christ as they meet together in doing the business of the church. Elder rule usurps the priesthood of the believer role because it denies the church members their right and privilege as believers to make decisions affecting the welfare of the church.[93]

As we come to the end of this chapter, I trust we have seen the church in a new light: as a gifted, capable, vibrant entity to

---

[93] Robert A. Wring, "Elder Rule and Southern Baptist Church Polity," *Journal for Baptist Theology and Ministry* 3, no. 1 (Spring 2005): 205.

whom most of the letters in the New Testament are addressed due to the responsibility and authority *inherent* in their calling as the body of Christ. We've seen the origin of the church's authority to "bind" and "loose" in Matthew 16, and observed the practical application of that authority in Matthew 18, Acts 1, Acts 6, Acts 15, and many other places throughout the New Testament. We've considered the important distinction between declarative and effectual authority, defined how leaders are chosen and appointed, and have seen that Jesus prohibits the church from operating with a hierarchical structure. We've also seen the power of unity in the church to manifest and testify to the very presence of Christ in a lost and needy world. Finally, I've tried to provoke you to remain diligent in your study of Scripture in order to understand more clearly doctrines like the priesthood of all believers and the authority of the church, for these doctrines guard us against spiritual abuse from authoritarian leaders and against false and heretical teaching.

As we study God's Word, it's imperative that each one of us in the body of Christ develop our own personal convictions on these important matters. We must ultimately become convinced of the truth by the Holy Spirit. This happened in my own life when God brought me through profound crisis, disillusionment, and desperation to a place of peace and freedom where I personally discovered these wonderful truths. Developing my own convictions about these critical doctrines eventually set me free from the tyrannical leaders and false doctrines I had previously embraced and helped me to discover the liberating truth and freedom that Christ offers to His people through the study of His Word.

As you grow in your own understanding on the critical issues presented in this book and develop personal convictions about them, you will experience a corresponding confidence and courage which will enable you to guard yourself and others from falling prey to the pitfalls of spurious teaching and abusive leaders.

In the next chapter, we will see how one individual, who recently helped expose one of the most heinous cases of sexual abuse in America, has now become a tireless advocate for victims of abuse throughout the evangelical church. Her insistence for justice and transparency has inspired confidence and courage in many others throughout the body of Christ to join her in holding church leaders accountable and seeking justice for victims of abuse.

# Study Notes

# 11

# THE VOICE THAT MATTERS

> *But we have renounced disgraceful, underhanded ways. We refuse to practice cunning or to tamper with God's word, but by the open statement of the truth we would commend ourselves to everyone's conscience in the sight of God.*
>
> —2 Corinthians 4:2

> *Of all work done under the sun religious work should be the most open to examination. There is positively no place in the church for sleight of hand or double talk. Everything done by the churches should be completely above suspicion. The true church will have nothing to hide.*
>
> —A. W. Tozer, *Of God and Men*

In January 2018, the court trial involving more than 150 young female athletes who were sexually molested and victimized by their doctor Larry Nassar came to a close. During his sentencing, the victims, for whom this case was agonizing, each gave a passionate "impact statement" that shared the profound effect that Nassar's actions had on their lives. These statements concluded with a sobering warning from a young woman named Rachael Denhollander, one of the many girls who had been sexually assaulted. I want to focus on a portion of her statement:

> This is what it looks like when someone chooses to put their selfish desires above the safety and love for those around them and let it be a warning to us all and moving forward as a society. This is what it looks like when the adults in authority do not respond properly to disclosures of sexual assault.... This is what it looks like when institutions create a culture where a predator can flourish unafraid and unabated and this is what it looks like when people in authority refuse to listen, put friendships in front of the truth, fail to create or enforce proper policy and fail to hold enablers accountable.[94]

According to witnesses in the case, a myriad of people holding leadership positions had enabled Nassar's abuse for years and sought to cover it up, and Denhollander recognized that the only way such a massive amount of sexual abuse could have continued for so long was through an unconscionable misuse and abuse of authority within a toxic culture that enabled that abuse to happen. Her observation is what I have been arguing

---

[94] "Read Rachael Denhollander's full victim impact statement about Larry Nassar," *CNN*, last modified January 30, 2018, https://www.cnn.com/2018/01/24/us/rachael-denhollander-full-statement/.

for in this book: that the root cause of spiritual abuse is *the misuse and abuse of authority*.

This, I am convinced, is why SGM had a class-action lawsuit filed against them with charges of sexual abuse similar to those of the Nassar case.[95] The misuse and abuse of authority is like the head of a poisonous snake—it is what precipitates and informs all other types of abuse. Its toxic integration into one's belief system is often the result of deception, intimidation, manipulation, brainwashing, mind control, and groupthink. Many ex-members of SGM acknowledge the enormous pressure imposed on them by their leaders to follow certain rules of behavior that were deemed to be SGM's standards for dating/courtship, marriage, child-rearing, and discipline—even participation in church activities and meetings. Sometimes these rules were clearly stated; others were simply implied. Either way, this *groupthink*, found in many evangelical churches, is a collective belief system which is also a principle characteristic of cults. While it may seem bizarre and abnormal to mainstream society, it feels completely normal to the affected members of the errant group. Groupthink helps explain mass suicides like Jonestown or Heaven's Gate and mass weddings like those of the Unification Church.[96] Clearly, falling prey to deception can lead to dire consequences.

Both of these malevolent behaviors—misusing authority and covering up abuse—work symbiotically to accomplish the same deplorable outcome, where perpetrators are left unaccountable for their actions and protected from civil authorities,

---

[95] For more information on the SGM case, please see the websites listed at the end of this chapter.
[96] Steven Hassan, *Combatting Cult Mind Control* (Rochester, VT: Park Street Press, 1990), 80–81.

and victims are silenced and told by leadership to keep the matter private. Some victims, even after being abused, continue to comply with an order of silence because they have already been indoctrinated into a skewed understanding of spiritual authority. They believe their leaders are to be unconditionally obeyed. Sadly, grave consequences result whenever an individual or congregation allows this to occur.

In contrast to these silent voices, Rachael Denhollander, two years before the Nassar trial, seized an opportunity to speak out against injustice in her own local church. Little did she know, the effects of her actions would be felt throughout the evangelical community. An evangelical Christian herself, Denhollander for several years had been researching the myriad of unresolved allegations surrounding SGM[97] and the class-action lawsuit filed against the group for covering up sexual abuse in several congregations. When the former leader of SGM, C. J. Mahaney, was asked to speak at her church, Denhollander understandably raised concern, knowing that Mahaney had never acknowledged any failure to properly handle the allegations against him or his former organization. Denhollander herself did not hold any prominent position or title in her church but was simply a concerned church member who took seriously her responsibility as a follower of Christ to be involved in the affairs of her congregation. She rightfully *expected* her voice to be heard.

Unfortunately, she was ignored.[98]

---

[97] Rachael Denhollander, Twitter post, May 23, 2018, 8:14 p.m., https://twitter.com/R_Denhollander/status/999488694242463744.

[98] Joshua Pease, "The Sin of Silence," *The Washington Post*, May 31, 2018, https://www.washingtonpost.com/news/posteverything/wp/2018/05/31/feature/the-epidemic-of-denial-about-sexual-abuse-in-the-evangelical-church/.

It is very plausible that Denhollander had these unresolved allegations surrounding SGM in her mind as she read her closing statement to the court in the Nassar case. After the trial ended, she quickly began advocating for the alleged victims of SGM, challenging the organization to submit to an independent investigation—even offering to fund it herself. After all, she knew what it was like to be silenced and marginalized as a victim of sexual abuse in a toxic culture where leaders enabled and covered up that abuse.

From interviews with ex-members, Denhollander knew that SGM congregants were indoctrinated to believe their leaders had ultimate authority over them and would therefore be the only ones qualified to discern and decide difficult and controversial issues like sexual abuse. She also likely understood that such a culture of unquestioned obedience and submission was typically propagated from the pulpit by leaders whose arrogance overshadowed any responsibility to notify civil authorities and appropriately involve their congregations. Denhollander realized this could easily create a culture where, in her words, "a predator can flourish unafraid and unabated." In an interview with *Christianity Today* (CT), she revealed the personal cost and profound frustration of navigating the toxic culture of denial at SGM in her attempt to fight for transparency and accountability.[99]

> CT. In your impact statement, you say, "My advocacy for sexual assault victims…cost me my church."

---

[99] Morgan Lee, "My Larry Nassar Testimony Went Viral," *Christianity Today*, January 31, 2018, http://www.christianitytoday.com/ct/2018/january-web-only/rachael-denhollander-larry-nassar-forgiveness-gospel.html.

Can you share about when you decided to share with your church that you were going to speak up about this and what happened?

DENHOLLANDER. The reason I lost my church was not specifically because I spoke up. It was because we were advocating for other victims of sexual assault within the evangelical community, crimes which had been perpetrated by people in the church and whose abuse had been enabled, very clearly, by prominent leaders in the evangelical community. That is not a message that evangelical leaders want to hear, because it would cost to speak out about the community. It would cost to take a stand against these very prominent leaders, despite the fact that the situation we were dealing with is widely recognized as one of the worst, if not *the* worst, instances of evangelical cover-up of sexual abuse. Because I had taken that position, and because we were not in agreement with our church's support of this organization and these leaders, it cost us dearly.

When I did come forward as an abuse victim, this part of my past was wielded like a weapon by some of the elders to further discredit my concern, essentially saying that I was imposing my own perspective or that my judgment was too clouded. One of them accused me of sitting around reading angry blog posts all day, which is not the way I do research. That's never been the way I do research. But my status as a victim was used against my advocacy.

CT. Church leaders thought that your own experiences made you biased?

DENHOLLANDER. Correct. So rather than engaging with the mountains of evidence that I brought, because this situation was one of the most well-documented cases of institutional cover-up I have ever seen, ever, there was a complete refusal to engage with the evidence.

CT. Was this the SGM Ministries (SGM) scandal?

DENHOLLANDER. Yes, it was.

Fortunately, instead of being silenced by SGM leaders or intimidated by opposition from other high-profile evangelical leaders,[100] Denhollander found a national platform from which to advocate for victims of sexual abuse and expose the subsequent cover-ups that have become increasingly common in the American evangelical community as well as the Roman Catholic Church.[101] With regard to SGM, Denhollander has discovered exactly what thousands of ex-members already knew: any opinion or concern that jeopardizes the reputation of the organization would be met with denials, obfuscation, and vilification.

---

[100] Sarah Pulliam Bailey, "C. J. Mahaney Scandal: Evangelical Leaders Defend Pastor Accused of Sexual Abuse Cover-Up," Huffington Post, May 24, 2013, https://www.huffingtonpost.com/2013/05/24/c-j-mahaney-scandal-evangelical-leaders-defend-pastor-accused-of-abuse-cover-up_n_3334500.html.

[101] In August of 2018, an archbishop in the Roman Catholic Church has accused a myriad of church leaders, including Pope Francis, of covering up sexual abuse.

The ultimate reality that I live with is that if my abuser had been Nathaniel Morales[102] instead of Larry Nassar, if my enabler had been [an SGM pastor] instead of [MSU gymnastics coach] Kathie Klages, if the organization I was speaking out against was SGM under the leadership of [C. J. Mahaney] instead of MSU under the leadership of Lou Anna Simon, I would not only not have evangelical support, I would be actively vilified and lied about by every single evangelical leader out there.

The only reason I am able to have the support of these leaders now is because I am speaking out against an organization not within their community. Had I been so unfortunate so as to have been victimized by someone in their community, someone in the SGM network, I would not only not have their support, I would be massively shunned. That's the reality [brackets original].[103]

How does such an aberrant form of leadership and toxic expression of church culture ever find traction within a congregation? How does an organization of churches find itself inundated with horrendous accusations and ridden with scandal? Most importantly, why did these SGM congregations think they

---

[102] A former SGM youth group leader was charged with sexually molesting boys under his care.

[103] Kate Shellnut, "SGM Disputes Rachael Denhollander's Remarks," *Christianity Today*, February 6, 2018, http://www.christianitytoday.com/news/2018/february/sovereign-grace-rachael-denhollander-sgm-abuse-ct-interview.html.

weren't responsible to resolve such a grave situation? How did they become so impotent, weak, and ineffectual to the extent that they perceived themselves as having no bearing on something as serious as the cover-up of sexual abuse? Why did they accept a life of marginalization, subservience, and inferiority instead of being the primary arbiters and stop-gap measures of protection against such abuse? What accounts for their utter inaction when the care and safety of others was at stake?

The answer, as I've argued, lies in the misuse and abuse of authority. A perversion of spiritual authority, together with the methodologies implemented by abusive leaders and embraced by church members, has brought all manner of harm to the body of Christ. In cases of emotional or physical abuse, a victim typically *knows* that he or she has been harmed, regardless of the legitimacy of the perpetrator's authority in his life. For example, an abused child inherently knows that he has been harmed because there are bruises on his body, and he feels pain. Because of the harm done, he might be confused about the legitimacy of the perpetrator's authority, but this confusion does not negate the fact *that* he was harmed. In contrast, however, a victim of spiritual abuse *may or may not* realize that he has been harmed because he has likely been deceived into thinking that the perpetrator, usually a church leader, has biblical justification to require submission and obedience. Victims—even entire congregations—accept and embrace this deception to their own demise yet often do not experience the sting of spiritual abuse until later, after they have extricated themselves from their abusers.

Systemic spiritual abuse, precipitated by a perversion of spiritual authority, typically enables all other forms of abuse in the church. Sadly, many members of SGM have failed to raise their voices in defense—or even concern—of those who have claimed to have been sexually abused. Instead, they defend and support the refusal of SGM leaders to submit to an independent third-party investigation in order to expose the facts and restore honor and integrity to the name of Christ. As we saw in the previous chapter, this kind of unconscionable neglect comes from failing to understand two doctrines: the priesthood of all believers and the authority of the church. If we do not want to see similar behavior in our own churches, we *must* be good students of the Bible, ferreting out dubious teaching and abusive leaders in the light of Scripture. Otherwise, our whole congregation can find itself deceived.

Consider again Rachael Denhollander's warning as she addressed Larry Nassar and the rest of the court:

> This is what it looks like when the *adults in authority* [emphasis mine] do not respond properly to disclosures of sexual assault. This is what it looks like when institutions create a culture where a predator can flourish unafraid and unabated and this is what it looks like when people in authority refuse to listen, put friendships in front of the truth, fail to create or enforce proper policy and fail to hold enablers accountable.

What would happen if the kind of sexual abuse Denhollander experienced occurred at your own church? Who would be the "adults in authority"? The leaders? Or the entire congregation?

Our first inclination is telling. If we attend a church with a top-down structure where leaders make all the decisions and the laypeople have no effective power, then we would be inclined to point our fingers at the leaders and say *they* are the problem. *They* neglected to create or enforce proper policy. *They* failed to hold enablers accountable. However, if we attend a church where the congregation itself helps to ensure that adequate safeguards are in place in order to guard one another from frivolous accusations when warranted, as well as demand transparency, accountability, and justice when necessary, then such a church would be inclined to accept personal responsibility for the lack of safeguards that led to such abuse.

The apostle Paul was aware of the pitfalls of authoritarian leaders and passive, unengaged congregations, which is why he warned leaders against lording over church members and expected congregations to hold one another accountable, including leaders, in order to maintain unity and to be a compelling testimony of Christ to a watching world. Unfortunately, in contrast to this teaching, the leadership of SGM presumed to speak on behalf of its congregants when challenged by Denhollander and many other prominent Christian leaders to submit to an independent investigation in order to preserve and protect the good name of Christ. Instead of consulting their respective congregations, SGM leaders made an executive decision to refuse this request.

Denhollander wrote a public response, which I include here in full.

In a recent article with *Christianity Today*, I referenced deep concerns with the intentional failure to report sexual assault perpetrated in multiple churches by multiple elders at SGM Ministries (SGM), now "SGM Churches" (SGM). Three days ago, SGM responded to this article and stated I was "mistaken" in my statements and that these concerns "are not true and have never been true." They further stated that they would not respond to my "false accusations" with evidence as to why they are false because they would appear "unsympathetic" to victims of abuse. They linked, as proof, to the dismissal of the civil suit against them. The lawsuit was dismissed because the statute of limitations had expired. This is a dismissal on technical grounds only; it had nothing to do with the substantive claims made against SGM. It simply means that the time for which legal proceedings can be initiated has expired, and therefore the court no longer has the authority to examine the merits of the plaintiff's claims. Ultimately, this dismissal means that the evidence against SGM was never examined by the courts. This is not evidence, in any way, shape, or form, that SGM has not done what is alleged.

I am glad to know that SGM is concerned about victims of sexual assault, but

I assure them the most unsympathetic thing they can continue to do is refuse to respond to the concerns of sexual assault victims, myself included. I have no need to be protected from any evidence or response they have. On the contrary, I have sought out this evidence and a response for more than seven years.

I chose to pursue expertise in the area of sexual assault and institutional dynamics years ago, including my own legal training as an attorney. Having reviewed the allegations and evidence against SGM and their own responses to it, my concerns have only solidified and grown. I have summarized these concerns at the end of this post.

I am asking SGM to support their recent claim that I am making "false accusations," "mischaracterizing" [them] and communicating things that "are not true and have never been true," and instead show true care for the victims by finally dealing transparently with these concerns through taking one specific step:

Allowing GRACE, a Christian organization whose expertise is sexual assault and institutional dynamics, to do a thorough independent investigation of the organization's historical and current handling of abuse complaints, which will be released to the public.

GRACE has no affiliation with SGM or any survivors and therefore is in a unique position of approaching such an investigation with objectivity and independence. GRACE is founded and organized by Boz Tchividjian, the grandson of Billy Graham, and is comprised of a team of mental health experts, former prosecutors, and pastors who have a combined experience of over one hundred years of addressing sexual-abuse-related issues. Their legal knowledge, investigative abilities, and character is of the highest caliber. I will personally spearhead fund-raising efforts for such an investigation and donate myself to ensure that this can be done with no extra burden to SGM, if the organization will pursue transparency and accountability through GRACE. I will also readily accept any conclusions GRACE arrives at and personally and publicly apologize if I am found to be in error.

As SGM is not facing a civil lawsuit, there is no reason they cannot, at this time, pursue and provide answers to the many concerns, questions, and evidence about their handling of sexual-assault allegations. I am confident that the best way to care for past victims, and the best way to prevent assault in the future, is to take these steps. I hope to see them finally do so.

# THE URIAH SYNDROME

## *Summary of Concerns*

During a time when C. J. Mahaney was senior pastor of Covenant Life Church and in leadership in the parent organization he founded (SGM),

1. SGM had an internal policy of not reporting sexual-assault allegations to law enforcement and instead handling them internally. This is evidenced by statements made by multiple SGM pastors, including in official police reports and in internal SGM documents.
2. Elders in SGM churches did, in fact, follow this internal policy and did not report sexual-assault allegations, did not warn congregants of known sexual predators, and did not place limitations on known predators to prevent additional access to children. Under-oath testimony and police reports in criminal investigations demonstrate this.
3. Additional statements by numerous members of multiple SGM churches independently allege further conduct that is in line with known church policy and proven church practices, including failure to report abuse, failure to warn congregants of known predators, and failure to place limitations on known predators in

the congregation. These allegations are numerous, arose independent of each other, and are internally and externally consistent, all factors which carry substantial evidentiary weight.

4. Numerous independent victims and victim families allege that SGM pastors discouraged reporting, were uncooperative with investigators, interfered with investigations, or supported the perpetrator. Some of these allegations have documentary evidence, including a letter on church letterhead in the official court file in support of early release of a known pedophile. Other allegations should be given consideration because the allegations are numerous, independent, and internally and externally consistent.

5. SGM has never publicly acknowledged or repented of these known failures to report. They have never responded with specificity to any additional allegations that fit the known patterns outside of blanket statements that there was "no conspiracy" to cover up abuse and that the civil lawsuit was a threat to their First Amendment freedom.

6. Additionally, three of the elders directly involved in known instances of failure to report were close relatives of C. J. Mahaney, two brothers-in-law and a

> son-in-law. Internal church documents also state that every elder is to be notified of any claims of sexual assault. During many of the known and alleged failures, CJ was an elder in the church in question. Specifically, he was the head elder.
>
> These known failures and additional concerns and allegations merit close attention and an independent, transparent investigation by a trusted organization with expertise, if SGM wishes to show care for victims or prevent these failures in the future. I hope to finally see them take this step.[104]

I believe Denhollander is correct: an independent investigation of SGM will largely depend, as it did in her Nassar exposé, on the collective outcry and support from those in the shadows who find the courage to come forward and speak out. Abuse and control *must* be exposed to the light.

It won't be easy—victims often become disappointed, discouraged, and disheartened, thinking that justice will finally prevail, only to see their hopes dashed. That's why all survivors of abuse should make their voices heard through letters, e-mails, and interviews to whatever media source can share such stories. For victims of SGM in particular, Rachael Denhollander's story has become *our* story.

---

[104] Rachael Denhollander, "Response to Sovereign Grace Churches," Facebook post, March 1, 2018, https://www.facebook.com/notes/rachael-denhollander/response-to-sovereign-grace-churches/1720170721396574/.

Brothers and sisters, we have an opportunity before us for our voices to be heard—to come to the defense of victims of abuse and to make a difference for those in the next generation who are disillusioned and confused by what has taken place in the name of Christ during their lifetime. I pray that they will be witnesses to our diligent struggle to expose the misuse and abuse of authority in the church, to hold those accountable for wrongdoing, and demand justice for victims of abuse.

I know it's easy to feel that our efforts are insignificant and inconsequential. I know that we can feel overwhelmed when thinking about the challenging issues facing the church today. But we must not lose heart. We must not succumb to discouragement and apathy. Silence in the face of injustice, harm, and heresy will only ensure our demise. We dare not underestimate the voice that Christ has given to us: *the voice that matters*—the authoritative voice of the church!

\* \* \* \* \*

For more information on the SGM case, please visit the following pages:

- http://www.sgmsurvivors.com/stories/
- http://www.sgmsurvivors.com/lawsuit-info/
- https://www.thouarttheman.org
- https://world.wng.org/2018/03/a_time_to_speak
- http://video.foxnews.com/v/5753137912001
- http://www.christianitytoday.com/ct/2018/march-web-only/sovereign-grace-need-investigation-sgm-mahaney-denhollander.html

# Study Notes

# 12

## THE KEYS

*I will give you the keys of the kingdom of heaven, and whatever you bind on earth shall be bound in heaven, and whatever you loose on earth shall be loosed in heaven.*
—Matthew 16:19

*One generation shall commend your works to another, and shall declare your mighty acts.*
—Psalm 145:4

Anyone who witnessed the awesome outpouring of God's Spirit during the Jesus movement of the 1960s and '70s can attest to the exhilaration of seeing hundreds of thousands of young people swept into the Kingdom of God. Those memorable days clearly produced an abundant harvest for the Lord. At the same time, however, the Jesus movement also planted seeds of questionable practices and dangerous teachings, particularly from the Shepherding Movement, which germinated and matured into the pervasive weeds of spiritual abuse which continues to choke much of the evangelical church today. These nefarious teachings enabled, not just heavy-handed authority, but various degrees of brainwashing, manipulation, and mind control in which authoritarian leaders persuaded otherwise psychologically healthy church members to believe and behave in abnormal, unhealthy ways.

These atrocities have caused the shipwreck of many believers, and I too have felt the sting of spiritual abuse and harm born from my generation's failure to stop the pernicious *misuse and abuse of authority in the Church*.

Like generations before us, our contributions and mistakes will soon be left to posterity, and will fade into church history as we round the final turn in the great race we have endeavored to run. Soon we will pass the baton to the next generation. And while we may have fallen short at times as we gave our best effort; the opportunity still remains for us to convey something of eternal benefit and lasting encouragement to the young men and women eager to run with endurance the race set before them. As we pass this baton to the next generation, what will we place in their hands?

The transition from one generation to the next is an important one. Therefore, it behooves those of us who now pass the baton to humble ourselves where necessary and admit our mistakes. By doing so, we can provide strength, encouragement, and the example of humility to the next generation as we place into their hands a baton marked by wisdom gained from our mistakes as well as the benefits learned from the advance of the gospel in our generation. That is the reason I have written this book.

Still, much of the Church continues to suffer from various forms of abuse, particularly during the last fifty years. This must not remain acceptable. It is imperative we remember that the greatest assurance a church member has against falling prey to the error and subsequent harm of hyper-authoritarian leaders is the church itself (Matthew 18:15–17). Likewise, the greatest malady that can befall a local church is when the authority of Christ, manifested in a local congregation, is suppressed, subverted, replaced, or ignored. This is a grave error and typically a precursor for all manner of abuse to occur, including: sexual, physical, emotional, psychological, and spiritual abuse, as well as other harm and injustice. We must remember, it is the wise and necessary provision of God to every member of the congregation that insures that each one has unfettered access to the body of Christ to avail themselves of the congregation's counsel and judgement when necessary. For there is no greater authority in the church today than the authority represented in the assembled congregation. That is why Christ said to the church, "Truly, I say to you, whatever you bind on earth shall be bound in heaven, and whatever you loose on earth shall be loosed in heaven." *Matthew 18:18*

This is an awesome responsibility and a holy mandate we have as members in the body of Christ and we must be resolute in our resolve to ensure that a proper form of church structure enables care, correction, and reconciliation for every member in the church. Any form of polity or church government that does not concede ultimate authority to the congregation to govern itself, police itself, challenge unjust and abusive practices, have meaningful consideration in the selection of those who lead them, and to adjudicate church discipline, should be rejected.

Brothers and sisters, it is not a demonstration of love to neglect this duty. If we shirk this responsibility in the face of intimidating leaders or insist on maintaining peace at any cost, we will be complicit in our own demise, for abusive leaders can only exist when congregations enable them by failing to recognize and exercise the church's biblical mandate to implement reform where necessary.

It is time for the church to wake up and acknowledge that there is a systemic problem afoot which can only be diverted and remedied if congregations accept responsibility to behave like the body of Christ. We must embrace the empowering truth that Christ has equipped each congregation with gifts and callings resident in its members to take care of their own business.

I trust the material presented in this book has convinced those of us in the body of Christ that until we embrace the responsibility and authority given to the church by Christ, as God's sovereign means to mitigate harm and expose evil when necessary, all manner of abuse will continue to assail the church. If today's church is to stem the tide of encroaching evil that presses her from within and without, she must resolve to strengthen her feeble knees and stand firm and resolute as the stop gap measure against those things that would seek to destroy her. God's people must insist on reform.

In the final analysis, we must not point our finger solely at those in leadership as the source and blame for the church's problems. Ultimately, we must realize that the remedy for what ails the church is the church itself. Therefore, we must turn our finger around and point it at ourselves, collectively as the church, because that is where God points it. The *keys* (the authority of Christ in the church) have not been given to a pope, pastor, committee, council, synod, board, or any individual, regardless of their position or title. The power and authority of the keys have been given to the body of Christ! The question is, "What will we do with them?"

*The hand of the* LORD *was upon me, and he brought me out in the Spirit of the* LORD *and set me down in the middle of the valley; it was full of bones. And he led me around among them, and behold, there were very many on the surface of the valley, and behold, they were very dry. And he said to me, "Son of man, can these bones live?" And I answered, "O Lord* GOD, *you know." Then he said to me, "Prophesy over these bones, and say to them, O dry bones, hear the word of the* LORD. *Thus, says the Lord* GOD *to these bones: Behold, I will cause breath to enter you, and you shall live. And I will lay sinews upon you, and will cause flesh to come upon you, and cover you with skin, and put breath in you, and you shall live, and you shall know that I am the* LORD.

*So, I prophesied as I was commanded. And as I prophesied, there was a sound, and behold, a rattling, and the bones came together, bone to its bone. And I looked, and behold, there were sinews on them, and flesh had come upon them, and skin had covered them. But there was no breath in them. Then he said to me, "Prophesy to the breath; prophesy, son of man, and say to the breath, Thus, says the Lord* GOD: *Come from the four winds, O breath, and breathe on these slain, that they may live." So, I prophesied as he commanded me, and the breath came into them, and they lived and stood on their feet, an exceedingly great army. Ezekiel 37:1-10*

# Study Notes

# Appendix 1
# Exit Counseling from Spiritual Abuse

Exit counseling is the counseling model most often utilized when meeting with those who contact me for help. They typically find themselves in a spiritually abusive situation and want to get out of one, or they have already removed themselves from the abuse but have many questions regarding what happened to them and why. Exit counseling is similar to, yet distinct from, cult deprogramming, as Dr. Michael Langone, a psychologist who specializes in cultic groups, explains:

> Exit counseling is a voluntary, intensive, time-limited, contractual educational counseling process that emphasizes the respectful sharing of information with members of exploitatively manipulative groups, commonly called cults. Exit counseling is distinguished from deprogramming, which received much media coverage in the late 1970s and 1980s, in that the former is a voluntary process, whereas the latter is currently

associated with a temporary restraint of the cultist.[105]

Often, concerned family members initiate the first call for help regarding a loved one involved in an abusive organization. These family members play an important role in helping the abused individual seek help or meet with a counselor. Exit counseling is primarily an educational process whereby the counselor provides information to the abused individual that he or she would not otherwise be exposed to. The goal in this counseling is to facilitate a process whereby the abused individual's judgment is restored, and their self-efficacy (their ability to choose) is increased. The aim of this approach is to empower the individual to exit the abusive organization based on their own volition—not to pressure them into leaving the abusive group. In biblical terms, this kind of counseling that is focused on *information* is similar to the hope and promise of Scripture's assurance that "you will know the truth and the truth will set you free" (John 8:32). Indeed, I have witnessed the power of this simple truth prevail in the lives of many who previously were crippled by profound spiritual abuse, manipulation, and/or coercion. I hope those who currently suffer from spiritual abuse, or have a family member affected by abuse, always remember that there is powerful hope, encouragement, and liberty in God's Word, the Bible.

---

[105] Michael Langone, *Recovery from Cults* (New York: W. W. Norton & Co., 1993), 155.

# Appendix 2

# Scriptures Demonstrating the Authority and Activity of the Church Throughout the New Testament

In addition to the Scripture references located at the end of this book, this is a compilation of passages specifically demonstrating the authority and activity of the church. My hope is for this to be a convenient and concise resource to use when contending for the authority of the church in your local congregation.

### Matthew 18:15–17

> If your brother sins against you, go and tell him his fault, between you and him alone. If he listens to you, you have gained your brother. But if he does not listen, take one or two others along with you, that every charge may be established by the evidence of two or three witnesses. If he refuses to listen to

them, tell it to the church. And if he refuses to listen even to the church, let him be to you as a Gentile and a tax collector.

*The final court of appeal for church discipline is the church.*

## Acts 1:15, 21–26

In those days Peter stood up among the brothers (the company of persons was in all about 120) and said…"[O]ne of the men who have accompanied us during all the time that the Lord Jesus went in and out among us, beginning from the baptism of John until the day when he was taken up from us—one of these men must become with us a witness to his resurrection." And they put forward two, Joseph called Barsabbas, who was also called Justus, and Matthias. And they prayed and said, "You, Lord, who know the hearts of all, show which one of these two you have chosen to take the place in this ministry and apostleship from which Judas turned aside to go to his own place." And they cast lots for them, and the lot fell on Matthias, and he was numbered with the eleven apostles.

*The 11 apostles (the leaders) appealed to the 120 (the church) to select a replacement for Judas, a leader. The church put forward two candi-*

*dates from among their number and asked God to select one. The leaders then appointed/ratified that selection.*

## Acts 6:1–7

The saying pleased the whole multitude and they [the church] chose Stephen.

## Acts 11:22

The report of this came to the ears of [the church in Jerusalem,] and [they] sent Barnabas to Antioch.

## Acts 11:29–30

So [the church] determined…to send relief to [the brothers] living in Judea. And [the church] did so, sending it to the elders by the hand of Barnabas and Saul.

## Acts 13:1–3

Now there were in [the church] at Antioch… While [the church] was worshiping the Lord and fasting, the Holy Spirit said, "Set apart for me Barnabas and Saul for the work to which I have called them." Then after fasting and praying [the church] laid their hands on them and sent them off.

## Acts 15:22–34

Then it seemed good to the apostles and the elders, with [the whole church], to choose men from among [the church] and send them to Antioch with Paul and Barnabas. [The church] sent [two prophets]… And after they had spent some time, they were sent off in peace by [the church] to those who had sent them.

## Acts 18:27

And when [the teacher] Apollos wished to cross to Achaia, [the church in Ephesus] encouraged him and wrote to [the church in Achaia] to welcome him. When he arrived there, he proved to be of great benefit to [the church in Achaia].

## Acts 21:12

[The church] urged [Paul] not to go up to Jerusalem.

*This passage indicates it was not unusual for the church to assume they had influence on their leaders' decisions. It wasn't the elders trying to persuade Paul—it was the entire church.*

## 1 Corinthians 5:4–5

When you (the church) are assembled in the name of the Lord Jesus and my spirit is present, with the power of our Lord Jesus, you (the church) are to deliver this man to Satan for the destruction of the flesh, so that his spirit may be saved in the day of the Lord.

*Paul presumes that the issue of disciplining a member for sin is a matter to be handled by the entire congregation, not just those in leadership.*

## 1 Corinthians 6:3–5

Do you (the church) not know that we (the church) are to judge angels? How much more, then, matters pertaining to this life! So, if you (the church) have such cases, why do you lay them before those who have no standing in the church? I say this to your (the church's) shame. Can it be that there is no one among you (the church) wise enough to settle a dispute between the brothers?

## 1 Corinthians 7:1, 25, 8:1–4; 12:1; 16:1, 12

*In each of the above verses, Paul is answering questions that had been posed to him by the entire church. His responses are likewise directed toward the entire church.*

## 1 Corinthians 16:3–4

And when I arrive, I will send those whom [the church selects] by letter to carry [the church's] gift to Jerusalem.

## 2 Corinthians 2:6–8

For such a one, this punishment by the majority (the church) is enough, so you (the church) should rather turn to forgive and comfort him, or he may be overwhelmed by excessive sorrow. So, I beg you (the church) to reaffirm your love for him.

*Paul addresses the entire Corinthian church on how they should welcome an individual back whom they had previously disciplined through disfellowshipping/excommunication.*

# Appendix 3

# A Sample Letter to Your Congregation

The following letter emphasizes that every member in the body of Christ is subject to church discipline as taught in Matthew 18, including those in leadership. I include this as a template for you to use in your own efforts to argue for church authority within your own congregation.

My dear brothers and sisters,

I'm writing to humbly bring an urgent matter to your attention. The Bible clearly teaches that all Christians are subject to the discipline of Matthew 18. No one in the body of Christ is exempt. It is a loving and redemptive process—one our Lord has given us to sort out our differences when necessary and primarily to keep the church holy and in good repute, providing a compelling testimony to a watching world.

At [church/organization], laypeople have been removed entirely from this process. Instead, others who are not even members of that local body of believers are hired *without the authorization of the congregation* to assume a role only those in the local church should take. At the very least, the church should have the opportunity to address its own affairs.

It is reasonable for someone other than a local member of the church to help facilitate this process (at the church's bequest), but he is not authorized by Scripture to make any *ultimate decisions*. That is the responsibility of each particular local body of believers.

When a church neglects this responsibility, the consequences can be devastating. Brothers and sisters, God has provided everything necessary in our local church for the congregation to investigate, discern, and take care of its own affairs. Every gifting necessary to navigate these waters has been provided *by* Christ *for* the body of Christ. Jesus has tremendous trust and absolute confidence in the church to manifest His wisdom, counsel, and disposition regarding all the matters that confront a congregation. The problem is, *we have been taught otherwise.*

While there are several expressions of church polity that embrace the biblical principle of the church having the ultimate authority to manage its own affairs, we can't completely dismiss a principle that's clearly established in Scripture. If we do, it is at our own peril.

A congregation that refuses to embrace and apply one of the most important aspects of its ministry—church discipline—will eventually compromise its calling as a compelling witness of God to their surrounding community (John 17). When a church ignores these responsibilities and instead chooses passivity and denial, it is in danger of losing this witness to a watching world.

If our individual response to these recent revelations is to say nothing, do nothing, be passive and "let the leaders handle it," then we are effectively enabling poor leadership and shirking our responsibility as members of our local church.

This does not reflect well on our Lord and Savior Jesus Christ. The Bible says the church is the pillar and foundation of the truth. It portrays the church as robust, indwelt with the power and presence of Christ, and full of all the giftings necessary to manifest Christ's supernatural wisdom, counsel, and majesty on the earth. We are not to be a bunch of cowering, emasculated people who don't know how to judge rightly our own affairs as in 1 Corinthians 6:2–4. We are to reflect Christ's wisdom and authority, especially in the matters we face today.

I want to challenge each one of us to study the Scriptures. Don't allow our loyalty to the Word of God to be trumped by our allegiance to a certain way of doing church. Be a Berean. Drill down into passages that are relevant to the topic. At the very least, answer the following question: *does the church have authority?*

RISE UP, CHURCH! We need to get involved. We need to ask questions. We need to confront individuals, including leaders, where necessary and speak the truth in love. We need to insist that the church follow the course and remedy God has provided in His Word to handle such problems. We need to raise our voice and receive the mantle God has placed upon us as His holy people.

STAND UP, CHURCH! We are the pillar and foundation of the truth. We are not the body of Elijah. We are not the body of John the Baptist. We are not the body of Paul. *We are the body of Jesus Christ.* To be associated with the Name that is above all names should tell us something about who we are as believers. *We are the fullness of Him who fills all in all.* Let's act like it.

Your brother[/sister] in Christ

# Appendix 4

# Post-Traumatic Stress Disorder (PTSD) and Spiritual Abuse

### Abstract

The relevance of the American Counseling Association Code of Ethics, the American Association of Christian Counselors Code of Ethics, and the Diagnostic and Statistical Manual (DSM)-IV-TR is considered in relation to the spiritual component of individuals. Care of the spiritual component of the human being is a necessary and an important ingredient in maintaining a healthy constitution. Post-traumatic stress disorder and its symptomology are defined and explored. A definition of spiritual abuse is proposed, its various components considered, as well as the similarities in symptomology related to other abuses and traumatic events where victims of post-traumatic stress disorder are concerned. Remedies for spiritual abuse as it relates to PTSD are also discussed.

\*\*\*

This paper begins with the recognition by the American Counseling Association (ACA) Code of Ethics, the American Association of Christian Counselors (AACC) Code of Ethics, and the Diagnostic and Statistical Manual (DSM)-IV-TR that care of the spiritual component of the human being is a necessary and important ingredient in maintaining a healthy constitution. Next, an overview of post-traumatic stress disorder (PTSD) and its symptomology will be considered. Differential diagnoses will also be identified.

A definition of spiritual abuse will be proposed, its various components considered, as well as the similarities in symptomology related to other abuses and traumatic events where victims are often diagnosed with PTSD, such as those who have suffered physical or sexual abuse. Subsequent to defining spiritual abuse and providing the details of John's (pseudonym) experience of abuse, several proposed remedies for spiritual abuse as it relates to PTSD will be considered. Accordingly, this writer will explore abuse as it relates to the *potential* detrimental influence and power inherent in those who have the responsibility to care for and lead God's people.

While the term *spiritual abuse* may be an uncommon nomenclature related to PTSD, it is nonetheless very real in its symptomology and can be chronic, long-lasting, and extremely debilitating as a traumatic experience. This paper will consider PTSD as the principle or presenting diagnosis where profound spiritual abuse has occurred and will endeavor to demonstrate the appropriateness of diagnosing victims of spiritual abuse under the particular clinical classification of PTSD when severe abuse has occurred and the symptomology warrants such a diagnosis.

In view of the many spiritually abused individuals, this writer has encountered in numerous counseling situations over the past several years and the symptomology that has been most prevalent and consistent, a diagnosis of PTSD oftentimes seems most appropriate. For the purpose of this paper, a real-life victim's story of spiritual abuse will be utilized as a case study to demonstrate a PTSD diagnosis. His history, symptoms, and treatment will be noted accordingly throughout this paper. As noted previously, he will be anonymously referred to as John.

## Codes of Ethics and the DSM-IV-TR

Both the American Counseling Association (ACA) Code of Ethics and the American Association of Christian Counselors (AACC) Code of Ethics recognize the spiritual component of the human constitution and correspondingly acknowledge various maladies and interventions related to the spiritual dimension of an individual. Indeed, the ACA's (2005) mission statement asserts the following affirmation:

> The mission of the American Counseling Association is to enhance the quality of life in society by promoting the development of professional counselors, advancing the counseling profession, and using the profession and practice of counseling to promote respect for human dignity and diversity. (p. 2)

In the ACA's Preamble (2005), there is a succinct but similar affirmation, which ultimately effects the practical application of promoting respect for human dignity and diversity, namely "values inform principles" (p. 3). More pointedly, in section *A.9.a. "Quality of Care,"* the ACA Code (2005) specifically references the need for counselors "to take measures that enable clients to obtain high quality end-of-life care for their physical, emotional, social, and *spiritual* needs" (p. 5). Taken together, these statements acknowledge and give credence to the spiritual dimension of the individual and the need for corresponding diagnosis and treatment in addressing the spiritual dimension of our clients. These affirmations and exhortations, cited from both codes, combine to effectively acknowledge that even from a secular worldview, the spiritual dimension of the human being is an integral factor for counselors to recognize and consider when assessing, diagnosing, and treating various maladies of the human condition.

Accordingly, in the Biblical-Ethical Foundations of the AACC Ethics Code (2004), specifically in the Sixth Foundation, the code asserts, "The biblical and constitutional rights to Religious Freedom, Free Speech, and Free Association protects Christian counselor public identity, and the explicit incorporation of spiritual practices into all forms of counseling and intervention" (p. 6). Furthermore, in section ES1-300 "Informed Consent in Christian Counseling," subsection 1-331 "Special Consent for More Difficult Interventions," it states the following, "Close or special consent is obtained for more difficult and controversial practices. These include, but are not limited to: deliverance and spiritual warfare activities; cult deprogramming work; recovering memories and treatment of past abuse or trauma" (AACC, 2004, 1–331).

The Diagnostic and Statistical Manual (DSM)-IV-TR (APA 2000) as well recognizes the spiritual dimension with regard to potential problematic conditions that may be a focus of clinical attention. These conditions are referred to as V-Codes and are noted in Axis I on the DSM-IV-TR classification system (APA 2000, 28). Regarding the phenomenon of spiritual abuse, perhaps the most pertinent V-Code is "V62.89: Religious or Spiritual Problem" (APA, 25). However, because spiritual abuse and V62.89 "Religious or Spiritual Problem" are not considered a *subtype* or *specifier* related to any of the major classification disorders, they must be incorporated into one of the other DSM disorders for diagnostic purposes (i.e., post-traumatic stress disorder [PTSD], major depressive disorder [MDD], acute stress disorder [ASD], or other anxiety disorders).

## Post-Traumatic Stress Disorder (PTSD)

At the outset, this writer would like to acknowledge that other differential diagnoses may clearly be more appropriate as compared to the more extreme and life-threatening nature of PTSD (like suicide, etc). For example, in adjustment disorder, "the stressor can be of any severity…and occurs in response to a stressor that is not extreme (e.g., spouse leaving, being fired)" (APA 2000, 467). While one may be hard-pressed to imagine an individual being spiritually abused to the degree of meriting a PTSD diagnosis, this writer believes that the symptoms presented in this paper will justify the diagnosis of the more extreme disorder.

The classic symptoms and minimal requirements necessary for a PTSD diagnosis according to the DSM-IV-TR (APA, 2000) are as follows:

  A) An individual must have been exposed to a traumatic event in which both of the following occurred.

  (1) The person experienced, witnessed, or was confronted with an event or events that involved actual or threatened death or serious injury, or a threat to the physical integrity of self or others.
  (2) The person's response involved intense fear, helplessness, or horror. (p. 468)

At the time these events occurred in John's case study, John was an ordained pastor in good standing with the congregation. Over a five-year period, he was threatened with the loss of his job if he did not succumb to the wishes of several other pastors to relocate to another church. This involved manipulation, coercion, threats, and ultimately resulted in John being castigated and falsely accused of the "sin of wicked unbelief." John endured the misuse of church discipline (i.e., Matthew 18:15–17) and the embarrassment to him and his family from those who witnessed this unfortunate event. As a result, John experienced several anxiety attacks that escalated in their severity and frequency of occurrence. Eventually, he received a dual diagnosis by a licensed professional counselor (LPC) as having major depressive disorder and anxiety disorder NOS. At the time of diagnosis, John was suicidal, had lost forty pounds, and had experienced intense fear and helplessness, spending the majority of his waking hours alone in a dark room. His attending psychiatrist prescribed him an antidepressant, Xanax, for anxiety attacks and Ambien for insomnia.

Additional symptoms John presented that satisfied the diagnostic criteria for PTSD were "re-experiencing of the trauma, hyperarousal symptoms, and avoidance of stimuli that remind the individual of the traumatic event" (Maddux and Winstead 2008, 422). Other symptoms that correspond to a PTSD diagnosis are feelings of detachment or estrangement from others, sense of foreshortened future, irritability or outbursts of anger, difficulty concentrating, hypervigilance, duration of the disturbance/symptoms for more than one month, and finally the disturbance causing clinically significant distress or impairment in social, occupational, or other important areas of function (Kanel 2007, 195). These symptoms were undeniably present in John's case.

One of the saddest experiences this writer witnessed was when John was blamed for the physical, psychological, and spiritual condition he was in. As Kanel (2007) points out, this can lead to "feelings of shame, guilt, and suppression of the victimization" (p. 208). In John's case, the shame, guilt, and encouragement to suppress the victimization aspect of his abuse was largely a result of his friends and family, who had unfortunately believed the misrepresentations by the other pastors involved.

The symptomology of PTSD is also found in other victims of abuse, such as sexual abuse, physical abuse, and environmental disaster. Dr. Graham Barker (n.d.) affirms this phenomenon: "Most people understand the terms 'child abuse,' 'sexual abuse,' and 'emotional abuse' but find it harder to grasp the idea of 'spiritual' abuse. The task is easier when the definition identifies the common feature of all abuse—the misuse of power and privilege."

In fact, the presenting symptoms can be so similar that one would be hard-pressed to recognize the catalyst or origin of trauma in PTSD victims without ascertaining an accurate history and performing a thorough assessment of the client. Indeed, Wilson (2001) indicates that one of the most common and grievous features pertaining to all types of abuse, and one that lends itself to spiritual abuse in particular, is the component of families, friends, pastors, and churches *blaming and shaming* the victim for "his sin" or "spiritual deviance," and is represented in the following statement: "Perpetrator-defined reality is one of the distinguishing characteristics of all abusive systems, including family systems. Perpetrators choose this devastating deception in a pathetic, but usually successful, attempt to shift responsibility for sexual child abuse to the child" (p. 55). In John's case, the pastors endeavored to do the same.

While sexual and physical abuse cause profound trauma, spiritual abuse, because it constitutes the soul and spirit of an individual, profoundly affects one's understanding and perception of God. Perhaps even more damaging, as a result of their abuse, is the unfortunate and perverted perception of how the victim perceives God's view of themselves. The definition of spiritual abuse—its various components, motivations, and manifestations—will be discussed in the following section.

# Spiritual Abuse

*And he said, "Woe to you lawyers also! For you load people with burdens hard to bear, and you yourselves do not touch the burdens with one of your fingers."*
—Luke 11:46 (ESV)

Spiritual abuse is a real phenomenon that actually happens in the body of Christ. It is a subtle trap in which the ones who perpetrate spiritual abuse on others are just as trapped in their unhealthy beliefs and actions as those whom they, knowingly or unknowingly, abuse (Johnson andVanVonderen, 1991, p.16).

What constitutes spiritual abuse? The following definitions are cited to assist in understanding the key components and essence of spiritual abuse and how those who have been affected by it have come to experience and interpret its meaning in their own lives. To that end, Johnson and VanVonderen (1991) offer this definition: "Spiritual abuse occurs when someone is treated in a way that damages them spiritually. As a deeper result, their relationship with God—or that part of them that is capable of having a relationship with God—becomes wounded or scarred" (p. 13). The authors go on to state, "Spiritual abuse is the mistreatment of a person who is in need of help, support or greater spiritual empowerment, with the result of weakening, undermining or decreasing that person's spiritual empowerment" (Johnson and Van Vonderen, 1991, p. 20).

In John's case, he suffered the following atrocities at the hands of his abusers. These culminated in him experiencing what is commonly referred to as a nervous breakdown. The clinical diagnosis he eventually received from a psychiatrist was dual in nature: major depressive disorder and anxiety disorder NOS. After several years of pharmacological and psychodynamic interventions, a different clinician began to consider PTSD as a differential diagnosis due to the longevity of the psychopathology, sudden outbursts of anger related to his experience, and his anxious reaction at the prospect of going back into a church building.

A brief summary of some of the traumatic events that contributed to John's disorder(s) is being forced (job was threatened) by fellow pastors to say the words, "I have faith to go to [an anonymous city] to plant a church." Eventually, John agreed to go but came back to Richmond within four months due to his pronounced symptoms of anxiety and depression. Upon his return to the church from which he left, a "family meeting" was called, without him being present, where the third step in the Matthew 18 process took place: "tell it to the church" (Matt. 18:17, ESV).

During this "family meeting" of the church members, John was publically charged with a multitude of transgressions, some of which were desertion, wicked unbelief, selfishness, and pride, resulting in disqualifying him from ministry. John was also publically brought before the church he had just returned from to confess his "sins" before that congregation. He was also "required" to write a letter to all the pastors (approximately fifty) in this "family of churches" explaining his sinful behavior as the reason why he did not remain at the new church plant and was subsequently dismissed from ministry.

His fifteen-year friendship with the pastor who propagated these events effectively ceased to exist in John's life. This pastor was considered by John to be one of his best friends. The pastor's public rebuke of John resulted in the entire congregation abandoning and shunning him and his entire family. The culmination of these atrocities had the effect of causing resentment, anger, bitterness, and rage to reside in John's heart for several years afterward. Fortunately, through much biblically based counseling, John was able to genuinely forgive those who abused him.

Throughout this ordeal, John was discouraged from seeking professional help from a psychiatrist or licensed professional counselor, even when he became suicidal. He was also discouraged from taking medication, the pastors having convinced him that this was "sinful behavior." Needless to say, his wife and two daughters suffered vicariously from the trauma of these events and subsequently suffered profound anxiety and attachment issues. Eventually, they too had to avail themselves of counseling.

Typically, many factors contribute to an abusive culture. One of the most insidious values that is systematically taught and propagated in abusive groups and cults is the notion of *perceiving* the leader(s) or pastor(s) of the organization as "fathers." This can be done in very subtle and seemingly innocent ways but with devastating repercussions, especially when someone attempts to exercise his or her own volition or to make an effort to disassociate himself from that organization.

For example, the leader said to the congregation, "We are a big family. We are brothers and sisters in the Lord, and tonight I am going to speak to you as a *father* would to his children." Indeed, after one of these occurrences, this writer scheduled a meeting with the pastor who made such a statement and asked him, "If we are all brothers and sisters in the family of God, who do you perceive yourself to be in this family?" Without hesitation, the pastor responded, "I am the father." The Scriptures take issue with this notion and command us to "call no man your father on earth, for you have one Father, who is in heaven" (Matt. 23:9, ESV). As Sirkin (1990) points out, "Not coincidentally, many cults encourage this process by referring to the leader as 'father' or 'mother.' Family-like ties are nurtured among group members while contact with the 'old' family is discouraged. A quasi-paranoid worldview may discourage contact with the 'uninitiated' except for recruitment or fund raising purposes" (p. 120).

Temerlin and Temerlin (1982) also recognize this notion of using familial terms when members of abusive groups and cults refer to their respective groups as family, as in John's "family of churches." While this terminology may be perfectly innocent and without any manipulation or control intended, there remain groups and organizations that use the term to advance a subtle and spurious agenda, specifically to obtain and maintain authority and control over the members within the "family." Accordingly, Temerlin and Temerlin (1982) offers the following warning: "The major religious cults train recruiters to recognize depressed, lonely, and confused people; approach them and establish a warm and friendly relationship; encourage them to join a 'new family' based on love" (p.134).

Another behavior that is developed and fostered in abusive groups and cults is the practice of showering unusual amounts of affection and care on potential recruits and new members. Indeed, one of the most common experiences of those who are exposed to and eventually join abusive or cultic groups is a practice referred to as "love bombing." As the term implies, it is the exaggerated affection, care, hospitality, and sacrifice of time and effort directed toward those who are being wooed into the abusive group. What makes it very difficult in determining whether or not this behavior is indeed a precursor to abuse is that it is exactly the same behavior members of a healthy church are supposed to engage in (i.e., "love one another" [Rom. 12:10; Heb. 13:1]), "comfort those who are in any affliction" [2 Cor. 1:4], "show hospitality to one another" [1 Pet. 4:9], and many other similar exhortations).

The important distinction to be made is the *motivation* behind this behavior. For the former group, it is ultimately to gain loyalty, control, and authority over an individual, which eventually results in an abnormal and perverted dependence on others, particularly leaders. For the latter group, it is for the purpose of promoting the individual's spiritual health and freedom in Christ, with a view toward spiritual maturity, ultimately cultivating a greater dependence on Christ.

Sirkin (1990) describes many of the components of this ill-motivated behavior, stating that often those who proselytize the unsuspecting convey total acceptance, and offer the promise of friendship and meaningful, positive relationships. A childlike naivete is pervasive and encouraged. Suspension of critical thinking is encouraged and reinforced; one may be attracted to general ideas, such as "unification" or "world hunger" without being inclined toward critical evaluation. The decision to join, to become one of the group, is usually spontaneous and sudden. (p. 118)

Unfortunately, a common byproduct of the initial influence and effects of "love bombing" (exaggerated expressions of affection and acceptance by current members) is that members who are committed to such groups become very defensive, angry, and even hostile toward anyone who holds a contrary view regarding the group's genuineness and sincerity of care and love toward its members. Often, it is only when the individual decides to leave the abusive group or cult that they discover, quite quickly, that those whom they were convinced loved them unconditionally have now turned their affections and begun to shun and castigate them, privately and publicly.

This behavior is generally experienced by the victim unexpectedly and results in feelings of devastation, treachery, and betrayal. It is the profound impact that these experiences and feelings evoke that lends itself to the symptomology of PTSD by those who experience it. As many ex-cult members have testified, "I felt like my heart was being ripped out. Those whom I regarded as family members had abandoned me and left me by the wayside." Sirkin (2009) captures this phenomenon quite well: "The individual (cult member) is reluctant to hear anything negative about the group; it may be extremely difficult to convince him or her that the group has any but the best intentions" (p. 119).

## Treatment of Spiritual Abuse as a Component of PTSD

> *So I exhort the elders among you, as a fellow elder and a witness of the sufferings of Christ, as well as a partaker in the glory that is going to be revealed: shepherd the flock of God that is among you, exercising oversight, not under compulsion, but willingly, as God would have you; not for shameful gain, but eagerly; not domineering over those in your charge, but being examples to the flock.*
> —1 Peter 5:1–3 (ESV)

The apostle Paul, as well, speaking on behalf of his fellow leaders, reminded the church at Corinth of their ultimate objective as shepherds of God's flock: "Not that we lord it over your faith, but we work with you for your joy, for you stand firm in your faith" (2 Cor. 1:24, ESV).

Perhaps it would be helpful to explore the distinction between "legalism" and "lording over someone's faith." To say one is guilty of legalism is vague. *Legalism* is a noun. It does not necessarily connote specific action and tends to be ambiguous as a description of what someone did in order to constitute legalism. *Lording over*, on the other hand, is a verb.

It connotes that an action is being done to someone. In this writer's opinion, *legalism* is the fruit or result of an action. The action in this case is lording over an individual's faith. "Lording over" is the means by which leaders persuade or lead people into legalism by causing their faith to be applied to unbiblical actions, thoughts, and beliefs. Where spiritual abuse is concerned, lording over an individual's faith is often a precursor in establishing a legalistic culture, which in turn, leads to the practice of spiritual abuse.

Treatment of the spiritually abused individual is often a long and arduous process and necessitates extreme patience and perseverance on the part of the counselor, family members, and the other service providers. Sirkin (1990) offers prudent advice and possible treatment models that have proven to be effective:

> Treatment should ideally consist of two components: Family therapy and individual therapy. Exit counseling to help extricate the individual from the group may be indicated. The goal of the family therapy is to open lines of communication and move to the next stage in the family life cycle. The goal of the individual treatment is to enable a person to set and attain individual goals, different from the demands of a group, whether that group be a family or a religious community. Maladaptive personality styles should be identified and new patterns of behavior encouraged. Ultimately, the beliefs are less important than the ability

of the individual to choose freely personal goals and relationships. (p.122)

Several other treatment options for spiritual abuse as a component of PTSD have proven to be effective. The first intervention usually takes the form of crisis intervention. As Gladding (2009) indicates, "Crises often last in people's minds long after the events that produced them. Crises counseling as well as long-term counseling services are often needed, especially with individuals who have PTSD" (p. 22). This was certainly true in John's case. On several occasions, especially as the symptoms escalated from anxiety attacks to a major depressive disorder, the need for crisis intervention occurred often until a pharmacological intervention could be determined.

Once stabilized, John was able to participate in cognitive behavioral therapy (CBT), anxiety management training (AMT), and relaxation exercises. Maddux and Winstead (2008) confirm these three interventions as effective for individuals suffering from PTSD:

> The (CBT) protocol included exploration of irrational beliefs as well as (AMT) that included relaxation. Although objective measures showed no difference between the CBT group and control group, participants reported that they benefited from the cognitive therapy, AMT, and relaxation training. (p. 423)

One of the other common interventions for PTSD is to participate in group therapy. John did not have this intervention available to him. However, as Gladding (2009) points out, "Individuals in supportive group therapy report lower levels of subjective distress" (p. 424).

Woody (2009) also provides excellent advice to clinicians, therapists, and counselors when dealing with clients who have been maltreated by abusive groups. He recommends that they should

> actively explore their own biases about groups and the effects of these biases on current and former group members. Ultimately, they should challenge deception and abuse and evaluate the degree of social influence and the consequences of group membership, regardless of whether scholars or media call the group a cult. (p. 220)

Woody's (2009) point is an important one, in that it emphasizes the *process* of how one comes to be indoctrinated by such a group and not so much the common or cultural perspective regarding the stigma inherent in many cults and abusive groups. He wisely encourages therapists and counselors to "reject common misconceptions about group members and help clients better understand the systematic program of influence that may have brought them into their groups" (p. 227).

## Discussion

Fortunately, as was noted at the beginning of this paper and referenced by the two codes of ethics (ACA and AACC), an intentional recognition of the spiritual dynamic and dimension of the human constitution continues to be acknowledged and addressed in the field of mental health. New and innovative therapeutic techniques, models, diagnostic considerations, and treatment solutions are presently being researched and considered in the quest to offer relevant and therapeutic remedies to those who suffer from the malady of spiritual abuse. Witztum (2011) offers much hope in this regard:

> Over the last decade psychiatry and mental health professionals have started to employ a more holistic approach to mental health, which includes a consideration of clients' religion and spirituality. In the United States there are impressive data from a 2000 survey of US physicians regarding religious beliefs and practices and spirituality in clinical practice, that there is an apparent softening of what has been perceived as an anti-religious posture by psychiatry (Eichelman, 2007). The study affirms that psychiatrists, similar to the physician population as a whole, endorse the positive influences of religion and spirituality on health. (p. 1)

In keeping with Witztum's (2011) findings, this writer suggests that, as the professional mental health community recognizes the "positive influences of religion and spirituality on health," it would behoove that same mental health community to continue their efforts in exploring, researching, and addressing the needs of those who have been victimized by the trauma of spiritual abuse.

> *When the way is hard, the flock may often become quite unsettled, even when it's on its way home. The shepherd observes a poor old ewe, limping along at the tail of the mob. He goes to her and finds a small hard stick between her hooves. He takes the ewe in his arms, holds her gently and reassuredly, and carefully removes the offending hurt. He rubs in some soothing salve, lifts her to her feet, and moves her into the homeward path.*
>
> — John MacArthur

# REFERENCES

American Association of Christian Counselors. 2004. *AACC Christian Counseling Code of Ethics*. Forest, VA: American Association of Christian Counselors.

American Counseling Association. 2005. *ACA Code of Ethics*. Alexandria, VA: American Counseling Association.

American Psychiatric Association. 2000. *Diagnostic and Statistical Manual of Mental Disorders: DSM-IV TR* (4th edition). Washington, DC: American Psychiatric Association.

Barker, G. n.d. "The Insidious Harm of Spiritual Abuse." Christian Counsellors Association of Australia. http://www.ccaa.net.au/documents/SpiritualAbuse.pdf.

Gladding, S. 2009. *Counseling: A Comprehensive Profession* (6th edition). Upper Saddle River, NJ: Pearson Education, Inc.

Johnson, D. and VanVonderen. 1991. *The Subtle Power of Spiritual Abuse*. Minneapolis, MN: Bethany House Publishers.

Kanel, K. 2007. *A Guide to Crisis Intervention* (3rd edition). Belmont, CA: Brooks Cole.

Maddux, J. and Winstead, B. 2008. *Psychopathology: Foundations for a Contemporary Understanding* (2nd edition). New York, NY: Taylor and Francis Group, LLC.

Sirkin, M. I. 1990. "Cult involvement: A systems approach to assessment and treatment." *Psychotherapy: Theory,*

*Research, Practice, Training* 27, no. 1): 116–123. doi:10.1037/0033-3204.27.1.116.

Temerlin, M. K. and Temerlin, J. W. 1982. "Psychotherapy cults: An iatrogenic perversion," *Psychotherapy: Theory, Research, and Practice* 19, no. 2 (Summer 1982): 131–141. doi: 10.1037/h0088425.

Wilson, S. 2001. *Hurt People Hurt People: Hope and Healing for Yourself and Your Relationships.* Grand Rapids, MI: Discovery House Publishers.

Witztum, E. 2011. "Review of Religion and spirituality in psychiatry." *Mental Health, Religion & Culture* 14, no. 1 (January 2011): 79-81. doi: 10.1080/13674676.2010.535318.

Woody, W. D. 2009. "Use of cult in the teaching of psychology of religion and spirituality." *Psychology of Religion and Spirituality* 1(4): 218–232. doi:10.1037/a0016730.

# BIBLIOGRAPHY

"After Judge Dismisses Sovereign Grace Lawsuit, Justin Taylor, Kevin DeYoung, and Don Carson Explain Their Silence." n.d. *Christianity Today* online. Last modified July 22, 2013. https://www.christianitytoday.com/news/2013/may/after-judge-dismisses-sovereign-grace-lawsuit-justin.html.

Akin, Daniel. "The Single-Elder-Led Church." In *Perspectives on Church Government: Five Views of Church Polity*, edited by Chad Owen Brand and R. Stanton Norman, 25–86. Nashville: B&H, 2004.

Ambassadors of Reconciliation. n.d. "About Us." Accessed June 25, 2018. https://www.hisaor.org/web-content/AboutUs.html.

Bailey, Sarah Pulliam. "C. J. Mahaney Scandal: Evangelical Leaders Defend Pastor Accused of Sexual Abuse Cover-Up." Huffington Post. May 24, 2013. https://www.huffingtonpost.com/2013/05/24/c-j-mahaney-scandal-evangelical-leaders-defend-pastor-accused-of-abuse-cover-up_n_3334500.html.

Berkhof Louis. *Systematic Theology*. Grand Rapids: Eerdmans, 1996.

Blue, Ken. *Healing Spiritual Abuse: How to Break Free from Bad Church Experiences*. Downers Grove, IL: InterVarsity, 1993.

Brecht, Martin. *Martin Luther: His Road to Reformation, 1483–1521*. Minneapolis: Fortress, 1985.

Briggs, Megan "Rachael Denhollander on Fox: Evangelicals and Abuse." Church Leaders. March 29, 2018. https://churchleaders.com/news/321299-rachael-denhollander-on-fox-evangelicals-and-abuse.html.

Bruce, F.F. *The Book of Acts*. Grand Rapids: Eerdmans, 1988.

Carson, D.A. "Authority in the Church." in *Evangelical Dictionary of Theology*, edited by Walter Elwell, 249–251. Grand Rapids: Baker, 2001.

Chantry, Walter J. "The Christian Ministry and Self Denial." *Banner of Truth Magazine*, November 1979.

Clowney, Edmund. *The Message of 1 Peter*. Downers Grove, IL: InterVarsity, 1984.

Cowen, Gerald P. *Who Rules the Church?* Nashville: B&H, 2003.

"Covenant Life Polity Position Paper." *Reformed Churchmen* (blog), July 14, 2012. http://reformationanglicanism.blogspot.com/2012/07/sgm-saga-covenant-life-polity-position.html.

Denhollander, Rachael. "Response to Sovereign Grace Churches." Facebook post. March 1, 2018. https://www.facebook.com/notes/rachael-denhollander/response-to-sovereign-grace-churches/1720170721396574/.

———. Twitter post, May 23, 2018, 8:14 PM. https://twitter.com/R_Denhollander/status/999488694242463744.

Dever, Mark, Ligon Duncan, and Al Mohler. "Statement." Together for the Gospel. May 23, 2013. https://web.archive.org/web/20130606205256/http://t4g.org/statement/.

DeWaay, Bob. "Binding and Loosing: Part 1." *Critical Issues Commentary* 1, no. 1 (1992).

Downen, Robert. "Leading Southern Baptist apologizes for supporting leader, church at center of sex abuse scandal. *Houston Chronicle*. February 14, 2019. https://www.houstonchronicle.com/houston/article/Leading-Southern-Baptist-apologizes-for-13618120.php.

Downen, Robert, Lise Olson, and John Tedesco. "Abuse of Faith." *Houston Chronicle*. February 10, 2019. https://www.houstonchronicle.com/news/investigations/article/Southern-Baptist-sexual-abuse-spreads-as-leaders-13588038.php.

Eastwood, Cyril. *The Priesthood of All Believers*. Eugene, OR: Wipf and Stock, 1962.

Enroth, Ronald "The Power Abusers: When Follow-the-Leader Becomes a Dangerous Game." *Eternity Magazine*, October 1979.

———. "The Power Abusers." Apologetics Index. Accessed August 18, 2018. http://www.apologeticsindex.org/a08.html.

———. *Recovering From Churches That Abuse*. Grand Rapids, MI: Zondervan, 1994.

Ford, Wendy. *Recovery From Abusive Groups: Healing From the Trauma of Authoritarian Leaders*. Bonita Springs, FL: American Family Foundation, 1993.

Galli, Mark. "We Need an Independent Investigation of Sovereign Grace Ministries." *Christianity Today* online. March 22, 2018. https://www.christianitytoday.com/ct/2018/march-web-only/sovereign-grace-need-investigation-sgm-mahaney-denhollander.html.

Grudem, Wayne. *Systematic Theology*. Grand Rapids: Zondervan, 1994.

Hassan, Steven. *Combatting Cult Mind Control*. Rochester, VT: Park Street Press, 1990.

Johnson, David, and Jeff VanVonderen, *The Subtle Power of Spiritual Abuse*. Bloomington, MN: Bethany House, 1991.

Kraft, David. "Statement of Formal Charges and Issues by Pastor Dave Kraft." Patheos. May 10, 2013. http://wp.patheos.com.s3.amazonaws.com/blogs/warrenthrockmorton/files/2014/03/Statement-of-Formal-Charges-and-Issues-by-Pastor-Dave-Kraft.pdf.

Lambert, Steven. *Charismatic Captivation*. Real Truth Publications, 2003.

Langone, Michael. *Recovery From Cults*. New York: W. W. Norton & Co., 1993.

Lee, Morgan. "My Larry Nassar Testimony Went Viral. But There's More to the Gospel Than Forgiveness." *Christianity Today* online. January 31, 2018. https://www.christianitytoday.com/ct/2018/january-web-only/rachael-denhollander-larry-nassar-forgiveness-gospel.html.

Leeman, Jonathan. *The Church and the Surprising Offense of God's Love*. Wheaton, IL: Crossway, 2010.

MacDonald, Gordon. "Disciple Abuse." *Discipleship Journal* no. 30 (1985).

"Mark Driscoll Screaming How Dare You." YouTube video, 5:50. Posted by "JeremyMarriedGuy." April 8, 2009. https://www.youtube.com/watch?v=ZkaeAkJO0w8.

Miller, Samuel. *An Essay on the Warrant, Nature, and Duties of the Office of the Ruling Elder*. Philadelphia: Presbyterian Board of Education, 1832.

Mohler, Albert. "Statement from R. Albert Mohler, Jr. on Sovereign Grace Churches," (personal website), February 15, 2019. http://news.sbts.edu/2019/02/15/statement-r-albert-mohler-jr-sovereign-grace-churches/.

Mohler, Albert. "The Tragic Lessons of Penn State—A Call to Action" (personal website). November 10, 2001. https://albertmohler.com/2011/11/10/the-tragic-lessons-of-penn-state-a-call-to-action/.

Mohler, Albert. "The Wrath of God Poured Out—The Humiliation of the Southern Baptist Convention" (personal website). May 23, 2018. https://albertmohler.com/2018/05/23/wrath-god-poured-humiliation-southern-baptist-convention/.

"Mumford Repents of Discipleship Errors." *Charisma & Christian Life Magazine*, February 1990.

O'Connell, Patrick M and Morgan Greene. "Harvest Bible Chapel pastor James MacDonald fired." *Chicago Tribune*, February 14, 2019. https://www.chicagotribune.com/news/ct-met-harvest-bible-chapel-james-macdonald-turmoil-20190211-story.htm.

Orcutt, Ben. "Midlo Pastor Found Guilty of Soliciting Prostitution." *Chesterfield Observer* (Chesterfield County, VA), Aug. 26, 2015.

Paulson, Michael. "A Brash Style That Filled Pews, Until Followers Had Their Fill: Mark Driscoll Is Being Urged to Leave Mars Hill Church." *The New York Times* online. August 22, 2014. https://www.nytimes.com/2014/08/23/us/mark-driscoll-is-being-urged-to-leave-mars-hill-church.html.

Pease, Joshua. "The Sin of Silence." *The Washington Post* online. May 31, 2018. https://www.washingtonpost.com/news/posteverything/wp/2018/05/31/feature/the-epidemic-of-denial-about-sexual-abuse-in-the-evangelical-church/.

Piper, John. "Rethinking the Governance Structure at Bethlehem Baptist Church." Desiring God. Last modified April 27, 2000. https://www.desiringgod.org/articles/rethinking-the-governance-structure-at-bethlehem-baptist-church.

Prince, Derek. *Jubilee 1995 Celebration: 50th Year in Ministry.* Charlotte, NC: Derek Prince Ministries, 1995.

"Read Rachael Denhollander's full victim impact statement about Larry Nassar." CNN online. Last modified January 30, 2018. https://www.cnn.com/2018/01/24/us/rachael-denhollander-full-statement/.

Rosenthal, Philip. "How Bible Preachers Can Turn Into Cult Leaders." The Aquila Report. September 4, 2012. http://theaquilareport.com/how-bible-preachers-can-turn-into-cult-leaders/.

Saucy, Robert L. *The Church in God's Program.* Chicago: Moody, 1972.

Shellnut, Kate. "SGM Disputes Rachael Denhollander's Remarks." *Christianity Today* online. February 6. http://www.christianitytoday.com/news/2018/february/sovereign-grace-rachael-denhollander-sgm-abuse-ct-interview.html.

SGM Survivors. "Larry Tomczak's Story." December 2, 2011. https://www.sgmsurvivors.com/2011/12/02/larry-tomczaks-story/.

SGM Survivors. "Let's Help Ted Kober." Comment posted by "Unassimilated." October 8, 2001, 3:15 p.m. http://www.sgmsurvivors.com/2011/10/15/lets-help-ted-kober/.

Sirkin, Mark I. "Cult involvement: A systems approach to assessment and treatment." *Psychotherapy: Theory, Research, Practice, Training 27*, no. 1 (1990): 116–123. http://psycnet.apa.org/record/1990-17899-001.

Spurgeon, Charles. *The Metropolitan Tabernacle Pulpit*, vol. 7. Pasadena, TX: Pilgrim Press, 1969.

Stott, John R. W. *The Message of Acts*. Downers Grove, IL: InterVarsity, 1990.

Strauch, Alexander. *Biblical Eldership*. Colorado Springs: Lewis & Roth, 2003.

Weber, Jeremy. "C.J. Mahaney Breaks Silence on Sovereign Grace Ministries Abuse Allegations." *Christianity Today* online. May 22, 2014. https://www.christianitytoday.com/news/2014/may/c-j-mahaney-breaks-silence-sovereign-grace-ministries-sgm.html.

_____. "Lawsuit Claiming Church Conspiracy To Conceal Child Abuse Adds More Names and Charges." *Christianity Today* online, May 13, 2014. https://www.christianitytoday.com/news/2013/may/lawsuit-claiming-church-conspiracy-to-conceal-child-abuse.html.

"What the adulterer Tiger Woods needs to hear: from C. J. Mahaney." *The Domain for Truth* (blog). Posted by "SLIMJIM," December 10, 2009. https://veritasdomain.wordpress.com/2009/12/10/what-the-adulterer-tiger-woods-need-to-hear-from-c-j-mahaney/.

Witztum, Eliezer. Review of *Religion and Spirituality in Psychiatry*, edited by Philippe Huguelet and Harold G. Koenig. *Mental*

*Health, Religion & Culture* 14, no. 1 (January 2011): 79-81. https://www.tandfonline.com/doi/abs/10.1080/13674676.2010.535318.

Woolf, Bertram Lee. *Reformation Writings of Martin Luther*, vol. 1. London: Lutterworth Press, 1952.

Wring, Robert A. "Elder Rule and Southern Baptist Church Polity." *Journal for Baptist Theology and Ministry* 3, no. 1 (Spring 2005): 188-212.

# For Further Reading

Anyabwile, Thabiti. 2010. *Finding Faithful Elders and Deacons.* Wheaton, IL: Crossway Books.

Arterburn, Steve and Jack Felton. 2000. *More Jesus Less Religion: Moving from Rules to Relationship.* Colorado Springs: WaterBrook.

_____. 2001. *Toxic Faith: Experiencing Healing From Painful Spiritual Abuse.* Colorado Springs: WaterBrook Press.

Bridges, Jerry. 1988. *Trusting God Even When Life Hurts.* Colorado Springs, CO: NavPress.

Brauns, Chris. 2008. *Unpacking Forgiveness: Biblical Answers for Complex Questions and Deep Wounds.* Wheaton, IL: Crossway.

Burks, Ron and Vicki Burks. 1992. *Damaged Disciples: Casualties of Authoritarian Churches and the Shepherding Movement.* Grand Rapids: Zondervan.

Burleson, Wade. 2017. *Fraudulent Authority: Pastors Who Seek to Rule Over Others.* Enid, Oklahoma: Istoria Ministries.

Chrnalogar, Mary Alice. 1997. *Twisted Scriptures: Breaking Free from Churches That Abuse.* Grand Rapids, MI: Zondervan Publishing House. Revised edition copyright 1998, 2000.

Clowney, Edmund. 1995. *The Church: Contours of Christian Theology*. Downers Grove, IL: InterVarsity.

Cowan, Gerald. 2003. *Who Rules the Church: Examining Congregational Leadership and Church Government*. Nashville: Broadman and Coleman.

Cowan, Steven B. and Paul E. Engle (ed.). 2004. *Who Runs the Church?: 4 Views on Church Government*. Grand Rapids: Zondervan.

Dever, Mark. 2000. *Nine Marks of a Healthy Church*. Wheaton, IL: Crossway.

Dougherty, Michael Brenden. October 29, 2018. "The Case Against Pope Francis" *The National Review*.

Dupont, Marc. 2004. *Toxic Churches: Restoration From Spiritual Abuse*. Grand Rapids:, MI.

Flowers, Leighton. *The Potter's Promise: A Biblical Defense of Traditional Soteriology*. Evansville, IN: Trinity Academic Press, 2017.

Ganz, Richard. 2002. *Free Indeed: Escaping Bondage and Brokenness for Freedom in Christ*. Wapwallopen, PA: Shepherd Press.

Hart, Archibald. 1999. *The Anxiety Cure: You Can Find Emotional Tranquility and Wholeness*. Nashville, TN: Thomas Nelson.

Lane, Timothy S. and Paul David Tripp. 2006. *How People Change*. Greensboro, NC: New Growth Press.

Langberg, Diane. 2003. *Counseling Survivors of Sexual Abuse*. Xulon Press.

Leeman, Jonathan. 2016. *Don't Fire Your Church Members: The Case for Congregationalism*. Nashville, Tennessee: B & H Academic.

———. 2018. *The Rule of Love: How the Local Church Should Reflect God's Love and Authority*. Wheaton, Illinois: Crossway.

Orlowski, Barbara. 2010. *Spiritual Abuse Recovery: Dynamic Research on Finding a Place of Wholeness*. Eugene, OR: Wipf & Stock.

Packer, J. I. 1973. *Concise theology: A Guide to Historic Christian Beliefs*. Wheaton, IL: Tyndale, 1993.

_____. Downers Grove, IL: InterVarsity.

Piper, John. 1996. *Desiring God: Meditations of a Christian Hedonist*. Sisters, OR: Multnomah.

Platt, David. 2010. *Radical: Taking Back Your Faith From the American Dream*. Colorado Springs: Multnomah Books.

Singer, Margaret Thaler. 2003. *Cults in Our Midst: The Continuing Fight Against Their Hidden Menace*. San Francisco, CA: Jossey-Bass.

Streatfeild, Dominic. 2007. *Brainwash: The Secret History of Mind Control*. New York: St. Martin's Press.

Stout, Martha. 2005. *The Sociopath Next Door*. New York: Broadway Books.

Tozer, A. W. 2015. *Of God and Men: Cultivating the Divine/Human Relationship*. Chicago: Moody.

Tracy, Steven R. 2005. *Mending the Soul: Understanding and Healing Abuse.* Grand Rapids: Zondervan.

VanVonderan, Jeff, Dale Ryan, and Juanita Ryan. 2008. *Soul Repair: Rebuilding Your Spiritual Life*. Downers Grove, IL: Intervarsity.

Watts, Jack. 2011. *Recovering From Religious Abuse: 11 Steps to Spiritual Freedom*. New York: Howard Books.

Welch, Edward T. 1997. *When People Are Big and God is Small: Overcoming Peer Pressure, Codependency, and the Fear of Man*. Phillipsburg, NJ: Reformed Publishing Company.

Wilson, Sandra D. 2015. *Hurt People Hurt People: Hope and Healing for Yourself and Your Relationships.* Grand Rapids: Discovery House.

## For Help with Greek Translations

Bauer, Walter. 1979. *A Greek-English Lexicon of the New Testament and Other Early Christian Literature.* Chicago: University of Chicago Press.
Bromiley, Geoffrey. 1968. *Theological Dictionary of the New Testament, vol. VI.* Grand Rapids, MI: Eerdmans.
Moulton, James and George Milligan. 1976. *The Vocabulary of the New Testament: Illustrated from the Papyri and other Non-Literary Sources.* Grand Rapids, MI: Eerdmans.
*Novum TestamentumGraece.* 1956. Stuttgart: WürttembergischeBibelanstalt.

## Scripture References

| | | | |
|---|---|---|---|
| Exodus | 19:5–6 | John | 4:1–3 |
| | | | 8:32 |
| Numbers | 13:33 | | 10:27–28 |
| 2 Samuel | 11 | | 13:12-17, 34 |
| | 12:9 | | 14:26 |
| 1 Kings | 19:11–12 | | 15:12–13 |
| Psalms | 55:12–14 | | 17:20–21 |
| | 140:2 | Acts | 1:15–26 |
| | 145:4 | | 3:19–20 |
| Proverbs | 3:6 | | 6:1–7 |
| | 11:14, 24:6 | | 9:3–6 |
| Isaiah | 9:6 | | 10:34 |
| | 14:13–14 | | 11:22, 29–30 |
| | 41:10 | | 13:1–4 |
| | 61:6 | | 14:23 |
| Ezekiel | 34:4 | | |
| | 37:1–10 | | |
| Matthew | 5:14 | | 15:3, 22–23 |
| | 7:15–20 | | 17:10–11, 4 |
| | 16:13–19 | | 18:27 |
| | 18 | | 20:28 |
| | 20:25–28 | | 21:2 |
| | 23:1–3, 8–9, 15, 27–28 | Romans | 2:11 |
| Mark | 10:35–45 | | 8:11 |
| Luke | 11:46 | | 12:4–8 |
| | 25:25-26 | Galatians | 1:6-9 |
| | | | 3:1 |

|  |  |  |  |
|---|---|---|---|
|  |  | Ephesians | 1:23 |
|  |  |  | 4:4–16 |
|  |  |  | 5:25 |
| 1 Corinthians | 1:10, 13 | Philemon |  |
|  | 4:1, 16 | Hebrews | 6:20 |
|  | 5:1–13 |  | 7:26–8:7 |
|  | 6:1-8 |  | 12:1–2 |
|  | 7:1,11, 25 |  | 13:17 |
|  | 8:1–4 | James | 3:3 |
|  |  |  | 3:15 |
|  | 11:1, 33–34 | 1 Peter | 2:9 |
|  | 12:1–30 |  | 5:1–5 |
|  | 16:1, 3-4, 12 | 2 Peter | 1:3 |
|  |  |  | 2:1–3 |
| 2 Corinthians | 1:4, 23–24 |  | 2:5, 9 |
|  | 2:5–11 | Revelation | 1:5-6, 10 |
|  |  |  | 2:2 |
|  | 4:2 |  | 19:7–8 |
|  | 10:8 |  | 22:4 |
|  | 13:10 |  |  |
| Philippians | 2:5–8 |  |  |
|  | 3:17 |  |  |
| Colossians | 1:18 |  |  |
| 1 Thessalonians | 5:20,21 |  |  |
| 2 Thessalonians | 3:7–9 |  |  |
| 1 Timothy | 1:3–7 |  |  |
|  | 2:5 |  |  |
|  | 3:1–16 |  |  |
|  | 4:11–16 |  |  |
|  | 5:19 |  |  |
|  | 6:3–5 |  |  |

| | |
|---|---|
| 2 Timothy | 2:15 |
| | 3:16–17 |
| | 4:3–7 |
| Revelation | 1:5, 8 |
| | 1:6–9 |
| | 1:10,11 |
| | 2:7–8 |
| | 2:15 |

# About the Author

Bob Dixon is a licensed professional counselor (LPC) in the state of Virginia and has over thirty years of experience as a member of Sovereign Grace Ministries (SGM), currently named Sovereign Grace Churches (SGC), known to many as a heavy-handed, authoritarian church movement. Before leaving the organization in 2012, he spent approximately twelve years exposing and confronting spiritually abusive practices, he believed, were systemic to their organization and church culture.

As a result, Bob is able to understand and address many of the problematic issues that come from the *misuse and abuse of authority in the church* and how abusive practices manifest in the lives of their members. He has become very familiar with peculiar nuances often found in these types of churches and how they can result in problematic emotional, psychological, and spiritual issues.

Bob currently resides in Richmond, Virginia, with his wife, Marsha. He has a particular interest to serve as a consultant and counselor for congregations interested in implementing reforms in church structure and culture. He also has a passion to help the next generation establish vibrant house churches throughout the United States and beyond.

Connect with Bob through info@BobDixonLPC.com or visit BobDixonLPC.com.

CPSIA information can be obtained
at www.ICGtesting.com
Printed in the USA
LVHW030902150719
624095LV00002B/315

9 781644 718735